About the authors

Dona Witten is a management consultant with a background in computer and telecommunications technology. At present she is attached to Ernst & Young LLP, where she is consulting to automobile companies installing multi-million dollar computer systems. Thus she has responsibility for teams of up to 30 people. She is also an executive partner of Tara Associates, which advises on organizational change and optimisation. During the last few years she has acted as consultant to Echlin, IBM, Hunter Douglas, Cadbury and other similar companies. She is based in Ohio but travels all over the world.

Dr Akong Tulku Rinpoche was born in Tibet in 1939. He is an experienced and accomplished meditation master as well as a fully trained doctor in the Tibetan medical tradition. After the Chinese invasion of Tibet he lived in India for four years before moving to the UK and setting up Samye Ling in 1967, the oldest Tibetan Buddhist centre in the West. He now supervises many other such centres in Europe, Africa and Asia. At the same time he is president of ROKPA, an international relief organization operating in Tibet, Mongolia, China, India and Nepal.

Also available from Rider by Dr Akong Tulku Rinpoche:

Taming the Tiger: Tibetan Teachings for Improving Daily Life

Enlightened Management

TRANSFORMING YOURSELF
– AND THEN YOUR TEAM –
FOR MAXIMUM SUCCESS

Dona Witten
with Dr Akong Tulku Rinpoche

RIDER
LONDON · SYDNEY · AUCKLAND · JOHANNESBURG

First published 1998

1 3 5 7 9 10 8 6 4 2

Copyright © Dona Witten and Dr Akong Tulku Rinpoche 1998

The moral right of the Authors has been asserted in accordance with the Copyright, Designs and Patents Act, 1988.

All rights reserved. No part of this publication may be reproduced, stored in a retrieval system, or transmitted in any form or by any means, electronic, mechanical, photocopying, recording otherwise, without the prior permission of the copyright owner.

First published in 1998 by Rider,
an imprint of Ebury Press,
Random House, 20 Vauxhall Bridge Road, London SW1V 2SA
www.randomhouse.co.uk

Random House Australia (Pty) Limited
20 Alfred Street, Milsons Point, Sydney,
New South Wales 2061, Australia

Random House New Zealand Limited
18 Poland Road, Glenfield
Auckland 10, New Zealand

Random House South Africa (Pty) Limited
Endulini, 5A Jubilee Road,
Parktown 2193, South Africa

Random House UK Limited Reg. No. 954009

Papers used by Rider are natural, recyclable products made from wood grown in sustainable forests.

Typeset by SX Composing DTP, Rayleigh, Essex
Printed by Mackays of Chatham plc, Chatham, Kent

A CIP catalogue record for this book
is available from the British Library

ISBN 0-7126-7156-0

Contents

Introduction   vii

PART 1: *The Guide*

Enlightened Management	3
Taking Responsibility	11
Paying Attention	18
Introducing Yourself to the Tiger	26
Working with Emotions	37
Conflict	47
Competition: Winning and Losing	62
Limits	76
Riding the Tiger	91

PART 2: *The Exercises*

The Daily Exercises   105
Doing Nothing   105
Doing Nothing Too   107
Keeping a Journal   107
Working with Intense Emotions   109
Clarifying Blame   111

The Sequential Exercises   115
The Schedule   115
Breathing   117
Feeling   118
Golden Gate of Compassion   121

The Outer Elements	123
The Healing Lights	129
Holiday	134
'Positive'/'Negative' Contemplation	134
The Mirror	136
The Golden Potential Within	138
The Friend	141
The Enemy	143
Expanding/Contracting	146
Rainbow	148
Holiday	151
Review of the Outer Elements	151
The Inner Elements	152
Universal Compassion	157
Retreats and Support Services	161
Relaxation Retreat	161
Self-work Support Groups	164
Service Providers	164

Introduction

This book has come to exist for several reasons. First and foremost, because I have had the good fortune to have studied and worked for over twenty years with some truly remarkable people who are masters of the subject of this book. These people, my meditation teachers, have opened an extraordinary world for me. I owe them an enormous debt for the richness and meaningfulness of my life. They have taught me many things. But most of all they have taught me how to live, how to work with people, and by working with people to know myself.

They have taught me as much by example as by words and this book explains their extraordinary success in working with others – working with some pretty damaged people at that. These good friends just happen to be Tibetan Buddhists. But what they have to tell regarding how to live in harmony with yourself and fellow man transcends the bounds of any religion or culture. It speaks directly to common humanity.

Over the past twenty years I have watched these people work with their students, both Asian and Western. I have observed small groups of ten or twenty out of the population of an entire country become, over the years, organisations of literally hundreds of thousands, and at the centres of these organisations there are superb managers. It has not been easy for them. Their lives have not been without times of turmoil and conflict, nor without major setbacks and obstacles. But in each case, their perseverance has taught them how to resolve conflict through non-aggressive means. I have watched them bring harmony to situations that seemed to defy all peaceful resolution, and I have watched them grow and mature in the process. It seems that the more they have given of themselves to their work – their management tasks – the more they have grown as people and the happier they have become.

There is a special tool to help in such a quest, an exceptional meditation practice and text called *The Seven Points of Mind Training*, which is the basis for the content of this book. *The Seven Points* is not a modern book, in fact it dates back to the twelfth century, when Chekawa Yeshe Dorje, a Tibetan monk, composed the text from the teachings of the famous Indian scholar and meditation master, Atisha. What is remarkable about this text is that it is as fresh and vital today as it must have been 800 years ago.

The Seven Points is quite extraordinary, both for its wisdom and its brevity. Basically, it is a handbook on how to change daily life through meditation. It assumes that everyone is actively engaged in worldly activities and it uses those activities as the basis of a spiritual life. Indeed, the introduction points out that the greater the adverse conditions, the greater the opportunities through using these techniques. *The Seven Points* is not an instant guarantee of success, but it certainly helps to show an effective way forward and has informed much of the first part of this book. As much of the cultural trappings have been stripped away as is possible, leaving what is common to shared humanity: thus, it is not necessary or particularly useful to be Buddhist to gain something from *Enlightened Management*.

I have written most of this book while on my brief annual visits to Samye Ling Tibetan Centre in Eskdalemuir, Scotland. I first started my journey into Tibetan Buddhism here more than twenty years ago, and as far as I can tell, it hasn't stopped raining there yet. Samye Ling is important to me. I come back as often as I can – despite the damp, the mud, and the Scottish cooking. I come back here because of my teacher, Veneral Akong Tulku Rinpoche, a decidedly ordinary-looking, middle-aged Tibetan with a wife and three kids who also happens to be one of the most extraordinary managers of people that I have ever known. He, above all others, has shown me that peace and harmony are essential. And he has also shown me the truly miraculous work that people can accomplish when they do work in harmony. It is his work that is contained in the exercises in the second part of this book.

Dr Akong Tulku Rinpoche is a Tibetan doctor. He is also a reincarnate Tibetan Buddhist meditation master with hundreds of students, and the administrator of Samye Ling Tibetan Centre in Scotland, one of the largest Buddhist meditation centres in the world. In his 'spare time' he is the president of ROKPA, an international relief organisation whose motto is 'Help wherever help is needed' – that includes Tibet, India, Nepal, Britain, the USA and countless other countries where he has started clinics, hospitals, orphanages, schools, medical colleges, therapy practices and anything else that can help alleviate human suffering.

Needless to say, Dr Akong Tulku Rinpoche, or 'Rinpoche' as he is called, is an extremely good manager; he is also truly happy. He loves the work he does and the people he works with. Equally important, the people who work with him love and respect him in return. This is his book. He is the one who has taught me and others like me and it is his work that is being passed on here. It is entirely his exercises and philosophies that you will follow. This is his gift to you, no strings attached.

What he teaches about being an effective manager is not anything new. This is not something made up on the spot. The philosophies and techniques which are the basis for the exercises date back for centuries. Rinpoche's teachers taught him and their teachers were taught by others. The quest to become happy and successful managers is not a trail blazed in the wilderness but a very well-worn path walked by many feet. And some very worthy feet at that. This is the path of Dalai Lamas and Mother Theresas.

This book is designed as an *experiential* guide to enlightened management. The first two chapters set out the challenge, and then in 'Paying Attention' and 'Introducing Yourself to the Tiger' I introduce the 'Daily Exercises' of Part 2. The remaining chapters explore the particular demands of transforming your working life in depth. I suggest you read them through and then go back and work through them, perhaps when those issues come up for you. Or you may want to work with them before beginning the 'Sequential Exercises' in Part 2. The important thing is to allow yourself to explore these changes, not just read about them and understand them intellectually.

PART 1

The Guide

Enlightened Management

What makes you think work and meditation are two different things?
AKONG TULKU RINPOCHE

This is a book for people who want to be happy, fulfilled and successful. It is aimed primarily at managers, those whose goals are to get other people to work together harmoniously and profitably. There is an important reason for this. It is managers who most profoundly influence the happiness of workers as well as the profitability of business. Most people work in 'managed' environments. There is someone telling them what to do; and in turn they are telling others what to do. If you think this isn't the case, consider your own workplace. Who has the greatest potential for making your life heaven or hell? The chances are excellent that it's your immediate supervisor.

Countless careers and fortunes have been built determining what goes into being a good manager. Equally, as many careers and fortunes have been made determining the best ways to reconstruct the lives of successful managers and the people they manage. It is fairly safe to say that few people are perfect or even very good at being managers the first time around. It is a learned skill. It is something that has to be worked on.

Happiness versus Work

Everyone wants to be happy. Every man, woman and child on

this planet wants to be happy. It is, if you will, at the centre of what makes us human. Yet few would argue that in spite of this common goal, for the most part working lives are spent making oneself and fellow workers profoundly miserable.

As hard as they may try, few people can say that they are as happy or as fulfilled in their work as they would like to be. Nor can many businesses these days say they are as profitable or as well run as they would like to be. Quite often, when questioned about work experiences, employees respond that they feel frustrated and undervalued. They complain of a management indifferent to their needs, selfish, arrogant and out of touch with reality. On the other hand, management can often be heard to lament worker apathy and lack of motivation while at the same time complaining about its own feelings of ineffectiveness.

It comes down to this. Whether 'boss' or 'worker bee' or somewhere in between, people really aren't very happy working together. They don't like each other very much. They don't like the way they are treated and they are not particularly proud of how they treat others. Even when they do like each other 'personally', they often still find it extremely difficult to work together effectively.

It seems especially true that the perpetual tension between what is called 'management' and 'labour', boss and employee, is making the work environment into something closer to a combat zone than a place of co-operative effort. For the most part people work together not because they want to, but because they have to. Yet in spite of the differences, there is a common goal: everyone still wants to be happy.

Few of us believe, however, that happiness can be attained through work. Instead, we look for it in other ways – by turning to friends, say, or the values of family life. Sometimes exotic 'hobbies' and 'weekend warriorship' are explored, or there is a need for religion to enrich and give meaning to lives, filling that emptiness sensed at the centre. Work becomes only the means – namely money and status – to enable the pursuit of happiness somewhere else.

Of course, there are some people who do not give up on finding fulfilment in their work. These are the people who continue to work very hard to succeed. They spend long hours on the job, take self-improvement courses, get MBAs, search for excellence. Some of them do succeed. But is this success the same as personal happiness?

There are innumerable people who would contend that it is quite possible, even likely, for a person to be professionally successful without being personally happy: happiness has nothing at all to do with material success. On the other hand, they would also say that the pursuit of happiness without some consideration for the pursuit of material success is not very practical. Few have the desire or the means to abandon current responsibilities to 'go and find themselves'. There are families, jobs, children and that ubiquitous mortgage.

There is a belief that it is necessary to choose between happiness and professional competency and success; that a choice should be made between personal happiness and professional and organisational success. To this end, there is an inherent suspicion of successful people – and of happy people. And especially of happy, successful people.

Learning To Be a Good Manager

The business courses say that a good manager learns to work effectively with people to produce profitable results. A good manager also learns to manage his or her own time effectively. A good manager is known to 'walk around' quite a bit. A good manager, too, learns to inspire and lead. The list goes on and on. But the point is this: people learn to be managers. A set of behavioural traits and organisational skills needs to be learnt. These traits and skills come to form a kind of code language which is used to communicate with superiors, peers and employees. The shelves at the booksellers are full of advice on how to acquire and refine this language.

There is not much variety in this code language, however. For the most part, variations are possible only within a fairly narrow spectrum of options. It may be possible to adopt the Japanese paradigm, for instance, or opt for being a 'one minute' manager. For managers, especially middle managers, there is little deviance tolerated from the 'norm'. The word 'eccentric' is not often used when describing today's middle manager.

Some managers learn these lessons more easily than others and some, unfortunately, never learn at all. For most managers, this learning is essential to work effectively with other people in a business environment. The natural tendency towards self-centredness remains, however, making it virtually impossible to work effectively and co-operatively in groups.

Creating a Rift

As the lessons are learned, managers become 'professionals', covering up their 'natural selves' with layers of learned traits associated with the latest business management philosophy. They learn to wear suits on their bodies and they learn to wear suits on their minds. With the suits comes a gap – a gap between the professional self and the personal self. Most of the time, however, there is still that part that demands that it have its own way. Professional skills are used to manipulate the environment and the surrounding people so that the insatiable tiger of desire can be fed. When this doesn't happen, feelings are masked and for the most part it is forgotten that the inner self isn't particularly happy at work.

An enormous price is paid for maintaining this wall between the personal and professional selves. For some people, it becomes a medical problem. The symptoms of stress are well documented. There is little doubt that work can be a killer. It takes its toll on the body, ageing it faster than necessary, and people are left unable to enjoy the fruits of all that hard work.

Most of all, it is the mind and spirit that suffers, and relationships that break down. Just as business projects need hard work and time to develop, so do relationships. So much time is spent suppressing real feelings so that emotions won't get in the way at work, that in times of personal crisis – death, impending divorce, a child in trouble – it is difficult to know how to act or what to do. Sometimes the true self is so out of bounds that it is assumed that 'it's not our problem, it's the other person's.' Wives, husbands, children, friends are distanced so that it is no longer known what has been lost. So much effort and ambition are spent on developing the professional life that emotional and spiritual development atrophy. Managers may become giants of industry and commerce, but deep down inside all that remains are emotional and spiritual children.

But is this the only choice we have? Looking beyond the conventional business world, some of the happiest and most effective managers alive today are probably what are called 'holy people'. There are two especially well-known examples: the Dalai Lama and the late Mother Theresa. Both these remarkable figures became deeply involved in co-ordinating the work of teams of people; both won the Nobel Prize for their success in working with others. You don't get the Nobel Peace Prize for not getting along with people or not producing results. Most importantly, both of them manifested personal happiness and brought happiness to everyone around them (and in the Dalai Lama's case, still do so).

This does not mean that people have to become saints before they can become effective managers; nor is it necessary to hire and promote based on an individual's 'saintliness'. But there is a great deal that can be learnt about effective management from these people.

Looking for Solutions

It is not that managers aren't trying. They are all trying very hard. Books on business theory seem to be second only to diet books in their popularity. These books and seminars even seem to help for a while. Inspiration is sought and new goals set. Managers get out into the workplace; they communicate; they empower their workers; they build teams; they search for excellence; they do it all in a minute or less. And of course, they all use their Day Timers to keep track of it so nothing gets lost.

They do it for a while. But then it all begins to fade away. Once again, the joy is gone. Somehow or other, they revert to old habits, and most of all, there is no peace of mind. The gap that has developed between the trained professional self and the untrained personal self remains. This is why efforts at self-improvement have only short-term and superficial success. The very effort of 'self-improvement' only seems to heighten our awareness of the gap. We have accomplished nothing.

As long as emotional and spiritual needs at their deepest level are not acknowledged and the gap between the two selves continues unreconciled, no amount of self-improvement will make a manager truly happy. An untamed flurry of emotions and desires will continue to rage on the inside, resulting in unhappiness and frustration. Without internal harmony, external harmony in the work environment will be impossible and business will continue to be ruled by contention and inefficiency.

This does not mean that everything that has been learned about being effective managers should be abandoned. If everyone just said what they felt like, whenever they felt like it; if managers only worked when they felt like it and only with the people they liked, and fired the people who drive them crazy, it would soon be those managers who would be out of the door.

Most managers have spent an enormous amount of time and energy learning to become comfortable with the disparity between their professional persona and the inner person who still wants to feel loved and wanted, and who, above all else, wants to have his or her own way. Sometimes people even learn to forget that there is a gap at all. There is, however, a far better alternative. Managers who can understand the gap and overcome it can eliminate, or at least significantly reduce, tensions and increase their effectiveness. This is what this book teaches. It is not a 'how to *do*' book or a 'close your eyes and believe' book; this is a 'how to *be*' book. It is an outline of a spiritual process for self-awareness and self-fulfilment; a process of the heart and the mind. The key to this development is participation in the process. It is not the words that are so important; it is the integration of their meaning into a person's life. This meaning can be best, and perhaps only, integrated into a life through a whole-hearted participation in the process.

An Aside

Almost a decade ago I was with a gathering of people listening to the teachings of a very famous Tibetan Buddhist meditation master by the name of Jamgon Kontrul Rinpoche. It was a wonderful sunny, breezy day and there were hundreds of us assembled on a grassy lawn 'seeking wisdom'. A man close to me stood up and posed the following question: 'Rinpoche,' he asked in a somewhat defiant tone, 'I can understand that what you're talking about may be fine for Tibetans and other Easterners to follow, but it really doesn't have much to do with us Westerners, does it? Doesn't it make more sense for each of us to figure out our own personal paths to happiness rather than following your way of doing things? Can't we just borrow a few things from your tradition and continue doing what we're doing?'

The teacher grinned and spoke in his Indian-style English. 'How old are you?' he asked. A thirty-something number came back. 'Well then,' the teacher asked, still grinning, 'You've been trying for very long time to do this you way? No? Tell me then, have you made much progress?' A red face was the only reply. There was a great deal of sympathetic giggling from the rest of the audience. 'Now then,' the teacher continued, his face a bit more serious. 'What harm would it do to try it my way for little while and see what happens?'

Many of today's managers are very much like this man in the audience. They have been trying to do it their way for quite some time now. They have read every management book. They have listened to every self-improvement tape. They have tried the gym. They are taking their vitamins. And like this man in the audience, they haven't got very far – at least, not when it comes to being happy. They may be more successful (although probably not as much as they'd like to be), but they aren't really that much happier now than they were twenty years ago when they first started out.

Successfully Narrowing the Divide

There is an implicit understanding in society that lay practitioners, whatever their religious or spiritual inclinations, can never be quite as virtuous and holy as those who have taken monastic vows, precepts or ordinations. A truly spiritual life can't possibly be lived within the confines of fifty-hour work weeks. Work by its very nature taints spirituality. These beliefs are further confirmed by the lives of those religious leaders who have pursued the world of business and material accumulations with a little too much zeal, getting lost on the way. But it does not have to be this way. Living a spiritual life need not require a change of clothes and venue, and renunciation of the material world. Happiness and spirituality have nothing to do with monastic robes and clerical collars. Whether a person's 'job' is to pray for world peace or to set up the assembly line for next year's model change, it is who they are inside that counts, not what path is chosen for seeking personal happiness and the happiness of those around them.

A Dalai Lama doesn't work because he has to; he works because he wants to. He genuinely cares for other people and he wants to help them; it is the natural expression of his harmony with the world around him. Everyone can be the same.

Taking Responsibility

Drive all blame into one.
THE SEVEN POINTS OF MIND TRAINING

Even a cow can take care of just itself.
DR AKONG TULKU RINPOCHE

To most people, taking responsibility as a manager seems rather obvious. Managers are accustomed to taking responsibility. If they are ambitious managers, they are more than accustomed: they have learned to welcome responsibility. Responsibility is the mark of success; it is the way to get ahead; it is power.

Responsibility can take many forms. Mostly, however, managers are responsible for resolving complaints: the staff are unhappy with the new benefit package; colleagues can't understand why another part of the project isn't yet done; the supervisor doesn't see why everyone can't get along without another person on the team. A job can seem an unending struggle to keep people happy.

A complaint either implicitly or explicitly indicates a certain level of unhappiness. When people complain it is because they want something to be other than it is. They are unhappy or dissatisfied with a certain condition or event. Chogyam Thrungpa Rinpoche, a Tibetan meditation master, once described complaining as 'the squeal of ego having its toes stepped on'. A complaint associates an internal sense of unhappiness with an external situation. The assumption is that if the external situation improves, so too will the unhappiness.

Consequently, when people bring their complaints to their manager, that manager becomes responsible for their happiness. It becomes the manager's responsibility to transform the complaints into happy solutions. Success depends on how well the manager is seen to do this. Skilled managers, of course, are capable of going beyond merely reacting to complaints. They become sensitive to impending concerns and learn to anticipate and resolve them before they become problematical. Management books and seminars are full of techniques for managing complaints or for avoiding them altogether – or even manipulating them to advantage. Using these and their own personal experience, every manager develops mechanisms for complaint resolution. It is just another part of the business persona that is built up.

Of course, managers too have their complaints. Indeed, most people complain, whether skilfully or unskilfully. Complaints may be hidden so carefully that people are unaware of dissatisfaction. But the dissatisfaction remains. Inside, verbalised or not, everyone keeps a list of the complaints and blames that are keeping them from being happy and/or successful. 'If only the recession hadn't stopped me from starting my own business.' 'If only I had a different boss.' 'If only I didn't have to work for a living.'

But why do people complain in the first place? For most, the answer would be that there is a series of events and people standing between them and happiness and success. It is these external forces that are keeping them from being happy. But is this correct? Could it actually be because an inner sense of dissatisfaction has been mistakenly associated with an outer situation? Has a mistaken assumption been made that when the outer situation changes, the inner dissatisfaction will disappear?

While this may actually be true for a few brief moments with each occurrence, the larger truth is that complaints have nothing to do with dissatisfaction. If looked at closely, dissatisfaction has a life of its own. The complaints are only the symptoms, not the cause of unhappiness, and the happiness that comes from complaint resolution is exceedingly short lived. It never lasts. Almost immediately, minds turn to a new complaint or someone or something else to blame for dissatisfaction.

For many people, especially Westerners, it is difficult to accept that complaints are not actually connected to the objects of the complaints. In the East, it is different. Most Eastern cultures are accustomed to thinking in terms of karma and reincarnation. What happens in this lifetime is not the result of the vagaries of life but rather the result of good or bad deeds in this and previous lifetimes. Fortune and misfortune are the results of personal actions. If there is anyone to blame, it is only ourselves.

Taking responsibility is not a question of blaming oneself or others. It requires not so much that complaints are resolved, but that you commit yourself to getting rid of the underlying basis for complaint. As long as the desire to complain remains, whether skilfully dealt with or not, lasting happiness is not attainable. And as long as the resolution of internal dissatisfaction remains identified with the resolution of external events, any happiness attained will be fleeting at best.

However, a change in attitude towards complaining is not such an easy thing to accomplish or even to understand. Taking responsibility means resolving to understand that there is nothing to complain about and no one to blame, not even ourselves. Taking responsibility in its truest sense means taking responsibility for your happiness independent of external situations or events. It means taking responsibility for who you are and for who you will become. No complaints; no reasons for complaining.

Why Stop Complaining?

Here is a story that is in the repertoire of most Buddhist meditation teachers. It will help show why complaining is a negative attribute.

Imagine that you are standing in the middle of a wide, endless road. As far as you can see the ground is covered with sharp rocks and stones. Unfortunately, you need to travel down this road to get to where you want to go. Even more unfortunately, you are barefoot. It seems that you have one of two choices if you want to travel this road. You can either cover the road with leather, making everything smooth for your bare feet. Or you could use a little leather and make a pair of shoes for yourself and not worry about the stones in the road.

Modern lives are a lot like standing on that road. Many people are not happy with where they are. All around them the world seems to be full of stones and broken glass. There is a problem – and there is a choice. Either join the Leather Road Project and get going on paving the world with top-grain cowhide, or join the Leather Shoe Project and make a nice pair of efficient running shoes. Those who choose the second option, choose to change themselves, not the world.

The majority of people choose the Leather Road Project as their solution, preferring to seek to change everything around them rather than themselves. Many have been heavily involved with this project for as long as they can remember. They have even become quite adept at it, and are very efficient managers on the Leather Road Project. The problem is that they are having a little trouble finishing the project or even predicting when it will be done. Just when they think they are close to completion, they turn a corner and see more stones and broken glass stretching out in front.

In contrast, the people who have chosen the Leather Shoe Project are doing just fine. They don't care if the stones are sharp. They don't care how many stones are still in front of them. There is nothing to complain about. They are wearing their LSP trainers and they are dancing in the road.

It doesn't take more than a little reflection to see that there is something to be learned from all this. As long as there are going to be stones and broken glass in the world – and by all indications that seems to be highly likely – it is time to start thinking seriously about joining the Leather Shoe Project.

Getting off the Leather Road Project

As with all bad projects, however, getting off the Leather Road Project is not easy to accomplish. It takes a lot of work. Complaining and blaming habits can be strong and have probably been around since birth. It is not going to take just a day or a week to change. The transition begins by accepting that the world, and colleagues in particular, are not responsible for your personal happiness. It is not they who need to change.

At first glance, this seems a small thing, just accepting. But it represents a fundamental change in how you view the world and how you relate to other people. Rather than looking at your own life and the people and events in it as objects of exploitation, there solely for the purpose of your happiness, it is time to recognise that the world *reflects* rather than determines you. The most important element in this change is your relationships with other people. Everyone wants to be happy; everyone is in the same situation. Life's events are a shared experience of a mutual desire for happiness. Taking responsibility means not only accepting responsibility for your own happiness, but also for not hindering the happiness of others.

Managers are expected to get people to work together in ways that are beneficial to the organisations that pay their salaries. It is assumed that this will make everyone happy. The goal is only seldom achieved, and worse, only occasionally is it even taken seriously. Taking responsibility means not only committing to getting ourselves off the Leather Road Project, but also to making sure that everyone else has the same opportunity. Helping each other is the key to meaningful, joyful, successful work.

Changing this fundamental view of the world is not simply a matter of stating, 'I accept' and thinking that's that. Nor is this change a case of learning a new behaviour pattern. It is much more basic than that and much more profound. Taking responsibility for your own happiness is the first step in working compassionately with other people. Once colleagues are freed from the burdens of making you happy, they are freed of an enormous burden. When work is seen not as a matter of what is being gained or lost but rather in terms of what can be experienced for mutual benefit, opportunities are created for everyone to find their own happiness.

Resulting Happiness

The potential benefits are enormous. Complaining and blaming skew a person's judgement and the judgement of those working with them. They also take an enormous amount of energy. When complaints and blaming are reduced, more attention can be paid towards doing what is best for everyone in an organisation. Rather than the squeaky wheel always getting the oil, the opportunity exists to oil the wheel that *really* needs it.

When responding to the complaints of others with a new sense of responsibility, it also becomes possible to look beyond the 'message' and recognise if a larger unhappiness is present. You can become sensitised to the real needs of fellow workers and perhaps even to address those needs. In this way, a dramatic shift occurs in your relationship with work and with your colleagues. As the complaining and blaming diminishes, your attention shifts outwards to the needs of the organisation. Your role in relation to the people working alongside you becomes one of service rather than of being served.

To many people this can seem to be a message of personal renunciation and self-sacrifice – renouncing one's own happiness in favour of everyone else's. This is emphatically not the case. A new sense of responsibility does not mean a passive acceptance of whatever comes your way. Nor does it mean that a choice has to be made between personal happiness and the happiness of others. Quite the contrary. In taking responsibility for your personal happiness, you actually become less passive because there is no longer any need to wait for others to create happiness for you. Lives become freer as the self-imposed excuses for unhappiness are dropped. Creating opportunities for the happiness of others also leads to personal happiness because happy co-workers in turn create an environment in which it is easier for you to be happier. It is a self-enriching cycle.

This is new ground for most people and, like anything else new that we attempt, it is important to rely on the experience and guidance of those who have accomplished what you are now beginning to strive for. Luckily, such expert guidance is available. The exercises that Rinpoche has prepared in the second half of this book are designed to support you in this transformational process. As you work through these exercises, it is important to keep in mind that they all rest on the premise that you are responsible for your own happiness. They also rest on the belief that personal happiness is only possible when the happiness of others is valued equally.

In addition to the exercises that Rinpoche has prepared, his advice throughout this text about how people conduct themselves on a day-to-day basis is of equal importance. For together with accepting responsibility there is the matter of breaking free of old habits. You need to create opportunities to view the world with fresh eyes, unencumbered by the demands of conforming to conventional standards for happiness. You need to heal and reconcile the gap between your professional and inner selves.

Paying Attention

Always apply the remedy.
THE SEVEN POINTS OF MIND TRAINING

The problem with life is there's so little time for practice.
ZIGGY (A CARTOON CHARACTER)

Paying attention is the companion tool to taking responsibility. Together they form a relationship much like that between a piece of paper and a pencil. A piece of paper by itself can potentially be used to fold a paper aeroplane or an origami crane, but put it together with a pencil and the possibilities are far greater.

Most people assume that they know what is meant when they hear the words 'pay attention'. There is a sense of sitting up straight, listening carefully and otherwise being mindful of what's happening all around. Here the definition of paying attention is similar but even more basic. Paying attention means simply living in the present moment. It means being consciously aware of present events as they are happening. Nothing more. In fact, 'nothing more' is the essence of it.

For most people, a great deal of time is spent doing anything but paying attention. Much of life is lived recollecting the past or dreaming of the future rather than experiencing the present. The events of lives are remembered rather than being consciously experienced as they are happening. As events occur, our minds are often preoccupied with daydreams or anxieties rather than simply focused on what is happening here and now.

Our hopes for the future and our fears from the past condition our awareness, making it difficult for us to experience the present objectively.

There is a simple exercise that can be done to illustrate the point. As you sit reading this book, pause a moment and look out in front of you. Find some neutral object – a coffee cup, a picture or a plant. Rest your attention on this object, concentrating lightly, merely trying to be aware of the object. Then see how long it takes before your mind drifts off to thinking about something else. As soon as you become aware that your thoughts are 'somewhere else', return your awareness to the object in front of you. Repeat this process a few times until you get a feel for how your mind tends to drift off into the past or the future. This is how the vast majority of life is lived.

Rather than living in the present, most of what is done in life is habitual. People get up in the morning, take a shower, brush their teeth. They don't think about it very much, it is just what they do. The rest of the day continues in much the same vein. As a result, life has a greyness about it. Life isn't actually lived, rather the motions are gone through, the events remembered as vague dreams. Only the brief occasions of intense emotion – love, hate, anger, excitement – waken the mind.

Breaking the Habit

There are many habits that contribute to the greyness of life. One of the biggest, of course, is the Leather Road Project. For many, many people, this project has been around for so long that they don't even think about it any more. They are so busy with it that it is impossible to think of anything else. The problem comes when it is time to get off the project. The habit needs to be broken. This requires that attention is paid to what is being done.

There is another reason that paying attention is important. Many people may still not be convinced that the Leather Road Project is a bad habit. There is more than a little part of the mind that clings to it. So much of life's energy has been invested into it that it is hard to truly believe that so much time has not been wisely spent. In their heart-of-hearts they still believe that they can complete the Leather Road Project. This is their belief system.

Belief systems form in various ways. Generally, learning to believe something or accepting it as true occurs because in some way the truth is confirmed through experiences or by the experiences of someone who is trusted. Children only completely come to understand that stoves are hot when they get burned or nearly burned. As they grow older, they expand the scope of their belief systems by relying on the experiences of others whom they trust. It is not necessary to jump off the barn to believe that the vast majority of humans can't fly. Someone else's test can be relied on. A problem arises, however, when the right tests aren't performed. All the tests done in life, for instance, and which many, many people trust, indicate that the Leather Road Project is a good project. It's a mutual conspiracy. Until the right tests are done there is no way of proving that one project is better than another. This is where paying attention comes in. It is a means to directly observe what is happening in life and to make effective decisions based on those observations. Paying attention allows direct experience of both the Leather Road Project and the Leather Shoe Project. In this way, experiential knowledge can be gleaned regarding the qualities of each project.

As with setting out to learn any new task or skill, it is best to start slowly and simply and then gradually, as the process becomes familiar, move to more complex activities. It is best, too, to start with things that are familiar and with which it is possible to be comfortable. This applies to learning how to pay attention.

All managers are comfortable with, or at least resigned to, schedules and 'to do' lists. They are part of the management tool kit. A lot of attention is paid to the things that need to be done: lists are made and items crossed off. This time, however, we'll put a twist on a familiar tool – we'll use our time management tools to keep track of not doing anything at all.

How to Pay Attention

Time management techniques recommend that a few minutes are reserved at the beginning or end of each day to organise and prioritise for the time ahead. Paying attention is very similar – but also entirely different. Rather than starting the day with a list of things to do, start and end the day by spending some time doing absolutely nothing, using the exercises 'Doing Nothing' and 'Doing Nothing Too' on pages 105–7.

There is no specific form or set of topics for these daily reflection periods. But if there is a specific point that you wish to contemplate, such as a chapter in this book or a recurring emotional theme, use the evening session to explore it in relation to your present feelings and mental activities. This is your time; do what is most important to you.

Taking the previous chapter as an example, the reflection period might be begun by asking, 'What are the complaints that I have?' 'Do they have any relation to the way I'm feeling?' If the answer is at first 'no', then you might want to look deeper and see if this is really the truth. Reflect on the previous day's activities and see if and how these complaints have affected your relationships with people and events.

This process is not intended to be an epic soul-searching. That is not the mission here. Rather, it should be a gentle 'getting in touch', a making friends with yourself, as it were. At first, the process may seem heavy-handed and self-conscious but as you extend this practice over time you will find that it becomes more natural and effortless. Additionally, as you sensitise yourself to your emotional and mental states you will more easily be able to target those areas most important for your contemplation.

It is important to note that there is no right or wrong way to use this session. For each person the experience will be different. For those people who tend to suppress their feelings, it might be a sensitising experience. Alternatively, for those people who tend towards over-excitement, the effect may be calming and steadying. The important point is to feel a sense of relaxed freshness and a sense of lightness. This should not be a burdening process. You are not doing anything – anything at all.

After each morning session, you will find that you are now really ready to prioritise your activities and prepare for the day's work. Keep in mind, however, your previous reflections. Notice how your feelings temper your priorities. Examine your 'to do' list in terms of what is really important. Do your scheduled tasks reflect your own complaints and the complaints of others, or do they truly reflect what is best for everyone? You might find your priorities changing slightly.

Developing Paying Attention

It is likely that your morning session will be the last time for calm reflection until the end of the day. The rest of your time will be spent busily moving from one activity to another. It is time to learn to pay attention the rest of the time when there is no opportunity for quiet reflection. This involves learning to be in the present as things are happening. Just as you learnt how to hold an object in attention, now it is time to learn how to hold life in attention. Learning how to do this is the key to overcoming the grey sameness that distinguishes most of life. It is time to wake up, even if for only brief moments at a time.

Since paying attention is not something that comes naturally, at first and for quite some time into the future, it will be necessary to remind yourself to pay attention. Use the twice-daily reflections as a starting point. Rather than immediately rushing into activities at the conclusion of each session, try to take the same relaxed attentiveness that you have just developed into the next activities of the day. If, for instance, there is a meeting scheduled, as you walk down the hall try to be aware of your surroundings. Let your mind turn to your preparations but at the same time keep part of yourself in balance. As you begin to talk to people, try to keep your awareness, rather as if there were another person standing slightly behind you watching the process. This experience, of 'being two people', is likely to develop naturally as you begin to pay attention.

Don't be surprised if at first you utterly fail to do this. In the beginning, you will most likely discover that you have gone through an entire day without even once paying attention. It may be only when you sit down in the evening for your scheduled reflection that you remember that you should have been paying attention. It is here that there is an opportunity to be creative. Everyone needs to find ways to remind themselves to pay attention throughout the day. There are countless ways in which the challenge can be approached. Classical Buddhist texts say that everyone should pay attention at four times – on standing up, eating, going to sleep, and waking up. Look for a similar approach. If you use a day-planner, for instance, you might write yourself a note, 'noon: pay attention'. When you see this note, whether it is noon or not, take a moment – perhaps look out into space and take a deep breath (not while you're driving!) Collect yourself – perhaps reflect a moment on the thoughts and feelings of the morning's session. For just a moment, try to do absolutely nothing. Then continue with whatever you were doing, trying to maintain your attentiveness. If circumstances allow, and it's not too irritating for you or your colleagues, you might want to use a watch or clock which can be set to beep every hour or half hour. Each time you hear the beep, come back to paying attention. You might also use certain activities as a cue. Shopping and queuing, for instance, are perfect opportunities for paying attention. Rather than reading the headlines on the tabloids, just stand there and do nothing, nothing at all. Train yourself, too, to remember to begin your attentiveness each time you walk into a new room or a building, then see how long you can maintain your awareness. Use your imagination. Be creative.

Developing the skill of paying attention can be expected to proceed in fits and starts. It will go something like this: you will remind yourself to come back to the present; you will, for a brief moment, be aware of events as they are happening; then you will lose your mindfulness in a storm of activity until something again reminds you, perhaps much later, to pay attention. Most of the time you will still be asleep, but every once in a while you will wake up, even if just for a moment or so.

Eventually, as you continue with your reminders and with the exercises in the second section of this book, you may begin to develop a sensation of 'gap'. This is akin to standing back a half-step from yourself, observing your own actions. A certain dreamlike quality may also be present as well as a sense of airiness. This is not something to be concerned about or to particularly rejoice in; this is a confirmation of the effectiveness of the paying attention process. When it occurs, don't grab for it and don't be frightened by it. Just let it be.

Paying attention may also take on another quality. Especially at the beginning, it may be impossible to be attentive in the 'heat of battle'. Things are simply happening too fast around you for any kind of relaxed reflection to be possible. Later, however, perhaps in your office after a particularly trying meeting with a staff member or supervisor, you may find yourself capable of reflecting on the events that have just occurred. You may also find that you can pay attention to the feelings you have as a result of the previous activity. This partial or incomplete paying attention will be useful later when learning to work with the true nature of your own emotional and mental constructs. For the time being, however, use this reflective time to figure out how to get out of the messes just created because attention wasn't being paid.

Walking on Eggshells

A caution about the Paying Attention process. At first, many people confuse paying attention with a mental construct most usually described as 'walking on eggshells'. This is when a manager has a predetermined concept of what appropriate behaviour should be and then commands him or herself to act accordingly. The results, while perhaps technically 'correct', are invariably stilted and phoney. What is gained in 'correct behaviour' (whatever that is) is lost in spontaneity, naturalness and, above all, tenderness. It is hard to like someone who is walking on eggshells. Somehow they just don't feel trustworthy. This is not what is meant by paying attention. Walking on eggshells is what has been done in the past. It is a trained management style. To a large extent, it is initially how the gap came about between the professional and personal selves.

Paying attention, on the other hand, has nothing to do with predetermined judgements about how people should present themselves to the world. It is not concerned with protection. There is no manipulation. It is true that there is the opportunity to choose to act differently in any given situation rather than merely reacting out of habit. But this choosing is done with a light touch as events are occurring. Additionally, because responsibility is now being taken for personal happiness, the world is not being manipulated for personal gain.

Paying attention also gives you the freedom to choose what to do and what not to do and what to say and what to leave unsaid, rather than being controlled by habit. In that moment before opening your mouth to speak, the possibility exists to think about what it is that you will say and how it will affect the people you speak to. Without paying attention there is no way to objectively measure the results of thoughts and actions both personally and on others. Without this assessment there is no way to improve in more than a hit-or-miss fashion.

The benefits of this process are enormous. For greater and greater amounts of time it is possible to push away the surrounding greyness and live in the present.

Introducing Yourself to the Tiger

My mind's got a mind of its own . . .
JIMMY DALE GILMORE

Be grateful to everyone.
THE SEVEN POINTS OF MIND TRAINING

Do the difficult things first.
DR AKONG TULKU RINPOCHE

When beginning to pay attention, the first thing you notice is yourself. You notice how you act and how you feel. You even begin to notice patterns, habitual tendencies, in the way that you act, or more precisely, react to certain types of situations.

You may be surprised by what you see. You may not like it. In fact, you probably won't be pleased at all. Most people will probably be so displeased that their instincts and consciences will propel them to immediately start changing themselves. Anything to improve on or hide what has been noticed. But before starting to change, take an even closer look. You need to first determine exactly where you are and where you want to be. You must get beyond your initial shock and truly investigate who this stranger is. *Then* you can think about change.

One of the first things that is suspected when first starting to pay attention is that this stranger is a consummate liar, and on many, many levels, too. Everyone undoubtedly lies to other people – to some degree that happens all the time; but they also lie (in fact, even more so) to themselves. With the ability to pay attention comes the discovery that you aren't really who you pretend to be – to others or to yourself.

One of the lies is that of the business persona, the projection presented to the world. As paying attention develops, you begin to see beyond the 'civilised' shell presented to others. And this is worrying. Maybe someone else can see beyond that persona too. Maybe the emperor isn't wearing any clothes. This results in panic. A business management course is taken; the anxiety attack is allayed. The manager holds him or herself even more aloof from colleagues. True feelings are suppressed even deeper.

But it is important that this instinct is resisted. The pattern of feeling has been exposed but then the situation is 'corrected' by hiding behind yet another personality projection; the habitual solution of the Leather Road Project. As paying attention develops, it is impossible not to notice the potholes in the Leather Road. It is important, however, that the urge to expend all your energy filling them in and paving them over is resisted. Somehow, the courage and determination to live with the discomfort must be found, at least for a while, so you can take advantage of the 'exposure' to take a good look.

This is not a particularly comfortable situation. The Tibetans have a saying for the level of self-awareness that comes with paying attention. It is like the difference between how a hair feels in the palm of your hand and how the same hair feels in your eye. Westerners have a saying too: 'Ignorance is bliss'.

It is perhaps strange to talk about learning to be a more effective manager in terms of bravery and courage. Brave people aren't usually associated with temperature-controlled offices. But it is these qualities that need to be cultivated. If you are brave enough, this discomfort and anxiety can be used as a further motivation to get completely off the Leather Road Project. As you progress through the exercises in Part 2, resist the urge to hide from yourself as much as possible. Everyone already knows that you are not wearing clothes. Stop worrying so much about it. After all, they're not wearing any clothes either.

There is a difference, however, between bravery and stupidity. No one wants to suffer or make themselves needlessly miserable. Pain for its own sake is not brave, it's stupid. The purpose of not hiding from yourself is not to hurt or punish. That has already been mastered. The purpose is to understand the nature of the disease and then to find the appropriate cure. And as quickly as possible. Think of the discomfort that may arise from paying attention as a reminder to take the medicine. Nothing more.

Once awakened to the symptoms of the disease, it becomes possible to discover the root causes and ultimately to cure it. The first step is to go beyond the lies and find out who you really are and what you want. It's not easy. The problem with lying, especially when it has been going on for a long time, is people usually forget where the lie ends and the truth begins. Somewhere in the 'professionalism', the true, inner self has got lost. Reasoning doesn't help much. People's minds are very, very slippery. As Akong Rinpoche has said, 'We can't think ourselves to enlightenment'. This is a situation where intellectual determination alone isn't enough to get beyond the projections. Being cleverer won't necessarily make you happier. And it certainly won't make anyone else happier. So something else needs to be tried, or at least something in addition to what is already being done.

Making Progress

Now that you are learning to pay attention you will be experiencing a small amount of mental and physical well-being. However, you may also be experiencing a fair amount of frustration. As much as you may have wanted to calm your mind and pay attention, you have probably had the experience that most people have; rather than calmness, your experience is more like being confronted with a wild tiger in a cage. It is hard to get past the flurry of thoughts and emotions and get to your real feelings; the mind keeps slipping away. Sometimes it may have seemed that fifteen minutes' more sleep would have been more useful. You have probably noticed, too, that the more agitated your mind is, the more difficult it is to settle down in a contemplative frame of mind. There seems to be a direct correlation between mental calmness and the ability to think clearly.

For further proof of the relationship between calmness and clear thinking, pause to remember the last time you were in a particularly heated argument with someone – the kind of argument where no one was interested in compromise or reasoning. Remember what it was like when everyone was yelling or launching heat-seeking missiles across the conference table. It was only after everyone began to calm down a bit and relax, that some objectivity could be brought to the situation and a solution could even be considered. As long as everyone was upset, objectivity wasn't possible. Before looking at your own mind with some degree of objectivity, you too need to learn how to calm down a bit. Until then, self-explorations will be more like trying to reason with an hysterical child.

The approach for learning how to calm down is like a mother's approach to calming that hysterical child. Any mother will say that screaming or pleading with a child to stop crying is not a particularly effective way to resolve the problem. Sometimes an indirect approach is more effective. A little love and soothing will work where a threat won't. You need to treat yourself in the same way and learn how to be really kind to yourself. This involves learning how to relax and be soothed. In particular, it involves dealing with the tension that most people live with on a daily basis.

Learning How to Relax

The exercises already suggested for the beginning and end of each day can be an effective means of relaxation, especially if additional attention is placed on the breathing sequence that begins each session. To be effective, however, it is important to do them conscientiously each day. For some people this may be the only relaxation available for an entire day, or maybe even the whole week.

All the exercises in Part 2 will partly help relaxation. Some of them, however, such as 'Breathing' (pages 117–8), 'Feeling' (pages 118–21), 'Golden Gate of Compassion' (pages 121–3), 'The Outer Elements' (pages 123–9), 'The Inner Elements' (pages 152–6), and 'The Healing Lights' (pages 129–34), are specifically intended for relaxation. It is important that you do them. Relaxation is the key to deriving benefit from the rest of the exercises.

Other means of relaxation are also useful. Taking exercise, walking in the woods, massage, drawing, driving in the country and aromatherapy are all useful means of sensitising and slowing down a bit. A word of caution, however, about sports as a means of relaxation. Many people carry their competitiveness and ambition on to the golf course and tennis court. Rather than being relaxing, games turn into wars. Smashing a tennis racket into the net post does not count as relaxation.

Everyone will have a slightly different definition of what it means to relax. For one person, a weekend camping can be a refreshing experience; for someone else, it can be a source of infinite boredom and mosquito bites. As you begin to know more about yourself you will discover that you can develop a feeling for when you need more or less relaxation and of what kind. One of the most important functions of the twice-daily contemplations is to gauge your own level of tension or relaxation and apply the appropriate remedies. Pay attention and be kind to yourself. Loving kindness starts with you.

As you learn to relax it is also important to keep in mind what you are trying to do. You are not trying to drug yourself into oblivion so that you don't have to deal with your problems. The importance of relaxation is that it makes work more effective. The activities chosen for relaxation should leave the mind refreshed and clear, not too tired or numb either physically or mentally. One more benefit is that as you relax you will begin to slow down a bit. And as you slow down you are able to see yourself more clearly. This is a good beginning.

Keeping a Journal

In addition to being slippery, the mind is selective about what it chooses to remember and how it chooses to judge events. Selective memory is the incubator for the business persona. To break the habit of lying, the ability to be objective about the past has to be learnt. To help with this, another component needs to be added to the evening contemplations: keeping a journal. This can be your planning book, an electronic wizard or a separate diary. Whatever is convenient for you. As you contemplate the activities of each day, preferably in the evening, take a moment at the end of each session to add a few notes to your journal. A description of how to keep this journal and the sort of things to write is given in Part 2 on pages 107–9.

Your first reaction to these suggestions of course will be, 'I don't have time!' Although the exercises and the contemplations are designed to take no more than half an hour to an hour each day, you may still feel that this is too much of an investment. This is why the journal is so important. This journal will very quickly become your motivation.

If you can't get yourself started with the relaxation exercises and the other exercises in Part 2, then at least do the journal entries. Commit yourself to keeping it for at least a month. Consider it an experiment. For now, the goal for keeping a journal is not to change behaviour; it is a way to better understand yourself, and especially to see how and why personal history is filtered. This is an attempt too to see where the lie starts. As you work with your journal, from time to time compare your current recollection of events to the notes that you recorded. Go back, especially to particularly sensitive areas, and re-examine an event to see how your memory of it has changed or been re-proportioned.

As you work with your journal, note, too, how the events of the past affect the way you act in the present. It is important to investigate this to understand how and why the business persona has developed. Watch for patterns. Be honest. You will undoubtedly recognise many things in yourself that you are not particularly proud of. At times it could become an overwhelming burden to carry around. But these exercises won't do much good if what is found leaves you incapacitated and depressed. No one has enough time to go to a clinic for a nervous breakdown. Nor should you be so terrified of what you might find that you lack the courage to look. So remember that as you do these exercises you are not looking for someone to blame. This isn't your mother's fault, your father's, or your gym teacher's. It isn't yours either. You are not looking for the 'truth'. There's nothing that you are trying to prove. There is no right or wrong answer. What you are doing is not a matter of judge and jury; it is a matter of medicine. You are doing this not to punish yourself, not to see what a terrible person you are. You are doing it to get to know yourself better. You are introducing yourself to the tiger.

Guilt is a very strong component of Western culture. It is regularly used to manipulate. But try to remember that everyone wants to be happy. As you look at the events of your life and the results of your actions, keep in mind that quest for happiness. Behind every event, look for the happiness that you thought you would gain. There is nothing wrong with wanting to be happy. As you review your journal entries each week, it is important to see the events in your life in the context of a quest for happiness. You need to look at each event and see how it relates to your own happiness – and how it relates to the happiness of others.

Working to the Core of Self

Relaxation now begins to take on a deeper meaning. Learning to relax with yourself means learning to accept yourself. Warts and all. It means acknowledging all of you; not just the parts that you like or that you want other people to see. It also means that you learn to forgive yourself for all your frailties and foolishness.

There is a very practical reason for learning to forgive. It is only then that the courage to stop lying can be found. The exercises in Part 2 are vital in helping to achieve this stage. Reasoning alone won't allow true relaxation. It is too hard to let go of the judging and blaming mind that insists on 'right' and 'wrong'. Instead, it is necessary to work with the mind on a deeper, more profound, pre-verbal level. The exercises are based on practices which are literally thousands of years old. They have been 'tuned' for Western culture, but in essence they are what has been practised by generations before. They work.

Have confidence in the effectiveness of the process. Otherwise, it is too easy to give in to despair and boredom and resume the lying once again. It is too easy to lose patience with the process and give up as soon as a particularly uncomfortable emotion or event is encountered. As you work with these practices, keep in mind that they are a centuries-old tradition. Being relaxed also means being comfortable in the knowledge that the journey is certain to lead to success. Be patient.

Taking Stock

Being relaxed in this way doesn't, however, mean becoming complacent about flaws and imperfections. If you are paying attention, there will be continual reminders of just how easy it is to hurt yourself and other people. It is important to look very carefully at life's events and decide which ones bring long-term happiness and which ones, no matter how temporarily pleasant they may be, bring unhappiness. This is like taking a personal inventory. It is your way to determine what is useful and needs to be strengthened and what is negative and needs a little transformational work. For each person this will be an extremely personal list. It will also most likely be a changing list as self-understanding deepens and broadens. Be as honest and thorough as possible. The more is known, the more likelihood there is of applying the right antidote for the disease. In this case, ignorance is *not* bliss.

The Benefit of Relationships at Work

During this review an incredibly exciting revelation will occur. So far, the approach has been very self-centred, almost claustrophobic, but now it is your relations with other people that reveal your true self in the most vivid detail. Relationships with other people, especially at work, are the best and quickest means to find out who you are.

People at work are particularly important because it is impossible to run away from them. Work forces everyone to deal with everyone else. Working with other people helps to expose strengths and weaknesses in ways that can never happen when working alone. When working with people, everyone is forced to face the peculiarities of their own personality. They are not allowed to indulge their own desires and stamp their feet and pout. They have to compromise. If you are paying attention and your motivation is correct, the daily events and the people you are working with can become an invaluable mirror.

Each evening as you review the day, think about your relationships with other people. Think about how you felt. Did someone make you feel small when they trivialised your work or left you out of an important decision? Yes? Then examine it. Look at your feelings. What was it that you wanted? And then ask yourself, 'Could I have discovered these things about myself without this experience? What if no one ever criticised my work? Would I understand how it feels to be belittled? Would I have the empathy for someone else in the same position?'

As painful as it might have been, recognise that this other person has given you a precious gift, one that you could never have discovered for yourself, or at least not nearly as quickly or as thoroughly. Even though the experience may have been comparable to a root canal, recognise how important this lesson was to your self-development.

It is always good manners to thank someone when they do something kind, even if they didn't mean to. While it may not be practical or sensible to walk up to the person who yesterday told you that you didn't know what you were doing and thank them for their opinion, for just a moment at the end of your evening session, send a thought of gratitude that person's way. Even if the pain or disappointment is too bitter at the moment to feel much sincerity, still make the effort. If necessary, come back to the experience at a later date when you review your journal. Perhaps then you can feel a little more sincerity.

As you work through the exercises in Part 2, something truly wonderful can happen. You can begin to look on other people with true gratitude. They are not the problem that you thought they were. They are the solution. They are the vehicles that allow you to see yourself more clearly. Without them you would never have the courage to find these things out for yourself. Working relationships encourage you to achieve things that you couldn't on your own.

There is a story that the Tibetans are fond of telling that illustrates this attitude towards work relationships. Atisha, the Indian pandit who first developed the mind training techniques being used here, was getting ready for his first trip to Tibet. Atisha, being not just a scholar but also a serious practitioner of mind training, was working hard to develop patience. To accomplish this he hired the surliest, foulest tempered Bengali teaboy he could find to accompany him on his lonesome and lengthy journey. What better way, he thought, to develop patience. The Tibetans take some perverse pleasure in noting, however, that within fifteen minutes of arriving in Tibet, Atisha realised that the teaboy was entirely unnecessary.

Everyone works with more than their fair share of Bengali teaboys. Rather than seeing them as obstacles to personal happiness, however, recognise such people and events as opportunities. In a sense, work becomes a testing ground, a place where you can keep trying until you get it right.

Although transforming our personalities is not yet a concern, the process of using work as a vehicle for self-discovery can't help but change our relationships with other people. Events can be recognised as opportunities to find out more. Difficult tasks and people need no longer be approached with dread. There is no need to avoid them or be defensive when they intrude. Because other people show you the true nature of your mind, it is possible to become profoundly grateful to them – especially when they cause mental upheaval. Instead of protecting yourself, it is possible to learn how to do what is appropriate for the situation; what is best for everyone. In this way, gratitude and compassion are developed naturally and spontaneously. Gratitude because people, especially those who differ, are like mirrors in which your true self can be seen; compassion because it is possible to empathise with others who are experiencing the same emotions.

With this recognition comes a new awareness of the value of work. Work is the laboratory, the testing ground, the hospital: everything that is needed to bring value into life. The more you focus on this, the more you can take advantage of the work experience. And the more progress you make with self-improvement, the more valuable work becomes. And when work becomes more valuable, its most important component – other people – will become more precious. And the more you value other people, the more effectively everyone will work together.

Working with Emotions

Work with the greatest defilements first.
THE SEVEN POINTS OF MIND TRAINING

Time heals all wounds.
PROVERB

It is now time to consider making behavioural changes. The personality most often associated with business is the cool, calculated exterior in total control of every situation. Controlled on the outside – charming even – yet raging with ambition and aggression just under the surface. It is understandable that it is difficult to give up this apparently successful model. But although it allows people to function with a certain amount of comfort, this is also exactly what is preventing them from being happy.

When a major change occurs in perception, it is called a paradigm shift. Western civilisation experienced such a shift when Columbus got lost and found the Americas – the world went from flat to round in an historical heartbeat. Perceptions changed dramatically. This is the stage that has been reached in this book. The rules are changing.

By now, your contemplations and your journal should be telling you a great deal about who you are and how you relate to the world. You should be realising the ineffectiveness and inappropriateness of your current ways of relating to other people and events. You should be seeing, all too clearly, what an incredible fake you are; how you hurt yourself and other people.

You may, of course, feel some fear and resistance towards the thought of change. When looking at yourself in the context of the world around you, you may feel that outwardly you are doing pretty well, both physically and materialistically. As the results of the relaxation exercises comes to fruition, it would be all too easy to look at what is being achieved and think, 'This is enough. I'm going to forget about the rest of it and stick with the old way of looking at things. Now that I'm more comfortable, I'm going to stay where I am.' But this state really is not enough.

Your contemplations and journal should also be revealing some of your limitations, giving you indications of the details of your behaviour patterns, and pointing out your greatest flaws, your greatest addictions. Of course, these traits are not necessarily the ones that are the greatest obstacles to professional success. But they are those characteristics that most prevent you being happy and also present obstacles to other people's happiness. These are the characteristics that must be worked with first. This involves working with one or more intense emotions or emotional patterns.

The First Steps

Many people cope with working with difficult emotions or emotional patterns by repressing them. Emotions cause trouble or create feelings of discomfort, so they are hidden by the business persona. But now is the time to find ways to work with emotions constructively, especially those that cause the most trouble. It is time to begin the process of taming the tiger.

One of the greatest obstacles to working with emotions is fear; fear of the unknown and fear of the unexpected. When beginning to work with emotions it is natural to feel afraid. It has been hard work caging that tiger, keeping her under control. There is so much to lose if all those efforts fail. But, ironically, the tiger has been breaking free and raising mayhem in the community on a regular basis. There is no cage that can ever be constructed strong enough or thick enough to keep her always locked up. It is time to negotiate.

One of our greatest fears is that of intense, uncontrolled emotion. Because we have not learned to work with emotions effectively, when we experience them, they tend to explode. Remember the last time there was an explosion of 'he said', 'she said'? Even with happy emotions, we tend to inadvertently step on the feelings of others as we revel in our successes. The sheer intensity of emotions becomes so self-absorbing that we lose touch with our surroundings and stop paying attention – and when that happens we make mistakes. So we need to find a way to work with these intense emotional outbursts when they occur. Don't be swept away by anger, greed, jealousy, passion. Learn how to minimise their impact. Then you can learn how to express your feelings constructively.

Of course many people will think, 'But I'm already doing that! I keep myself under control almost all of the time.' Repressing emotions is not the same, however, as learning to work with them. Even if emotions are kept under control there will always be times when they come rushing to the front, say during times of trauma – losing a job, experiencing a death, or dealing with the break-up of a marriage.

When strong emotions occur it is essential first to pay attention to them. Take time to work with your emotions; don't ignore them. You are already more in touch with your feelings simply because you have been documenting their eruptions but, when strong emotions occur, more needs to be done in the way of giving yourself space and time to experience what is happening. This may mean getting away from what you are doing; taking an hour or so away from work; going for long walks. Don't ignore your feelings or pretend they don't exist. It may be particularly difficult to acknowledge extremely painful emotions such as grief or anger constructively, but you can make a beginning by practising the exercise 'Working with Intense Emotions' on pages 109–11. Above all, don't ignore your emotions because you are fearful of them.

Contemplating the Past, Present and Future

In working with intense emotions, it is very important to pay attention to this next step: dealing with the reactions to intense emotions. Intense emotions tend to progress in something like an emotional chain reaction. Someone hurts you – perhaps betrays a confidence, or refuses to give you credit for your work. So you react, and to prevent more hurt, look for a way to protect yourself. Never again will you trust or even like that person. You build a wall to prevent the possibility of being hurt again. Then comes the chance to get back at that person, or someone similar. We retaliate: hurting someone in our turn. And then that person goes on to hurt someone else. And on and on it goes ... is it possible to get any work done?

Fear of emotional outbursts conditions behaviour more than is thought. In general, people and situations associated with intense emotional outbreaks are deliberately avoided. Much of the fear is a direct result of the fear of losing self-control. Even when it is someone else who is losing control, their reactions remind us of our tiger just barely caged and ready to escape. As a result, we tend to avoid emotion-prone experiences, even when it is more important to work with these experiences.

When working with intense emotions, especially those that are repeated as a pattern – rage and impatience, for instance – we need to find ways to break the cycle of cause and effect, and to avoid passing hurt on to others. There are two approaches to take. The first is to look at the past to see how your behaviour or attitude may have contributed to the pain you are feeling and the pain you are distributing to everyone in sight. This will help you to understand and forgive. It also helps you to recognise emotional patterns and so enables you to work with their root causes. The second approach is to observe your attitude and behaviour now and in the future. This helps break the cycle of suffering – an act of true compassion.

As you continue your sessions working with intense emotions, examine the past and the future with regard to the turmoil that you might be feeling. Looking at the past, examine the situation to see if there is something that you did out of foolishness or ignorance that contributed to the emotions that you are now experiencing. If there is, decide if it is worth continuing with the behaviour that resulted in your unhappiness. Looking at the future, it is especially important to determine how you can use your experience in a positive way to help both yourself and others.

Overcoming the Past

By learning to work with emotional intensity, you can overcome your fear of losing control. By working with the innate emptiness of emotions, even strong emotions, their manifestations, especially in colleagues, feel less threatening. Emotions are something to be transformed and clarified and harmoniously integrated into the quest for happiness. This is the key to understanding how to work with other people.

All intense emotions, good or bad, eventually fade from the forefront of consciousness. They do not, however, go away but change, even after their initial causes have long disappeared. All past experiences are carried around in some form or another. This emotional baggage continues to affect everything we think and do.

Unfortunately, this baggage is not something that you can easily get rid of. But there are several approaches that can help you work with it. The first involves the exercises in Part 2. There is not much value to be gained in merely reading these exercises; their real value comes in doing them. If you work with them regularly and progressively, they can be extremely helpful in healing the emotional scars of the past.

You can also use your daily contemplations and journal entries. Everyone has more than a few skeletons in their past together with a set of memories that, when recalled, cause winces of pain, embarrassment or anger. As your contemplations and journal entries progress, you may find these memories resurfacing, especially when encountering repeating emotional patterns. When this happens, most people's first tendency is either to rush into the feeling again – reliving, say, the self-righteous anger or the sheer joy of the moment – or to flee from the memory as quickly as possible. The remedy is somewhere between these two extremes. Most painful memories have some sort of blame associated with them, either blame directed towards yourself or blame directed towards someone else. Probably both. To help resolve these feelings, look at the 'Clarifying Blame' exercise on pages 111–4. The 'Golden Gate of Compassion' on pages 121–3 can also be particularly useful in learning to forgive your own mistakes.

Working with the Future

Now that you have some useful techniques for working with your emotional past and present it is time to explore ways to work with the future. You are ready to explore ways to interact with the people around you; to begin to choose how you treat people.

As you do your evening contemplations, you will most likely spend some time examining your feelings towards other people and the events of the day. If you are paying attention you will notice the beginnings of feelings, good or bad, arising out of relationships and out of the work that you are doing. While at the time these may have seemed like only minor irritations or emotional flirtations, in actuality, in many cases they were the seeds of emotional crises. Emotional obsessions such as intense likes or dislikes for another person, for instance, rarely arise full-blown in a moment. They develop over time. Little irritations fester and stew until they become international incidents. Miscommunications go unresolved until they become causes for glacial silence. Differences of opinion build and build until they become life-and-death struggles for dominance. This is not a pleasant way to live. It would be beneficial, especially from the perspective of our colleagues, if we could find a way to calm these emotional thunderstorms before they reach hurricane force.

There are many models for looking at our emotional patterns. Each of us is familiar with at least one method for analysing ourselves and other people. The Six Realms of the Buddhist tradition is one such way. You might find it an interesting alternative to labelling someone as affirming or controlling, for example.

The Six Realms

In working with emotional patterns it is convenient first to categorise them. This is a form of shorthand that can be used in describing behaviour and in applying remedies. There are several Western categorisations of human behaviour – A- and B-type personalities, for instance – that can be used, but this template from the Tibetan tradition is particularly insightful. Each 'realm' is ruled by a predominant emotional pattern. Every person, due to their past emotional experiences and other predispositions, tends to be predominantly from one realm or possible two. At any time, however (especially during tense business meetings), each person is quite capable of expressing behaviour associated with any or all of the other realms.

1. *The God Realm*
Primarily associated with pride, especially arrogance and a feeling of superiority. Those people who 'live' predominantly in this realm find it necessary to continually remind others of how wonderful they are. Quite often God Realm individuals are talented, which makes them even more difficult to deal with. Quite a few managers live in the God Realm. The problem with this realm, however, is that it leaves little space for anyone else. When working for a God Realm individual, others are perpetually reminded of how worthless they are. When there is a God Realm individual working for a manager, there are continual reminders that the manager doesn't really understand what needs to be done. If it wasn't for the God Realm individual, the department would come crashing to its knees.

2. *The Half-god Realm*
Primarily associated with jealousy and envy. Half-god Realm people are interesting to work with because they are always more concerned with their next job than the current one. They are continually convinced that they deserve more than what they have. Half-god Realm people never give up territory. We all become members of the Half-god Realm at promotion and review times.

3. *The Hell Realm*
Primarily associated with anger and rage. Hell Realm people compete. They are quite often consultants – primarily because they can't work in any one place too long without getting fired. What makes a Hell Realm person especially frustrating, apart from the discomfort associated with working with them, is that they seem to have a phenomenal capability for work.

4. *The Hungry Ghost Realm*
Primarily associated with a poverty and hunger mentality. Hungry Ghost Realm people always have an excuse. They always have a reason for their failure. Hungry Ghost Realm people have bad luck. Most people don't work for Hungry Ghost Realm people – they didn't get promoted because . . . . Most people, however, have Hungry Ghost Realm people working for them.

5. *The Animal Realm*
Primarily associated with stupidity and dullness. Animal Realm people hate change. They are quite often found as middle managers, especially in small companies or in departments without much change. Animal Realm managers are very stable and dependable. They won't surprise you very much. Animal Realm managers and employees always have their documentation done.

6. *The Human Realm*
Primarily associated with desire and frustration. While it's called the Human Realm, it isn't necessarily where everyone 'lives'. The Human Realm is associated with unhappiness and sadness. Human Realm people like change; they always want something different; they are always discontented. Human Realm people are more project-orientated than procedure-orientated – mainly because they are so restless that they can't do the same thing twice in the same way. Three times is sheer agony for them. Human Realm people make good consultants.

Each of the realms, and their countless combinations, has its own way of relating – both managing and being managed. The important thing is to use knowledge of the realms as a means to increase your understanding of how people tend to work with each other. Not being swept away by the drama of the emotions

WORKING WITH EMOTIONS

is the key to developing emotional balance.

In addition to your day-to-day observations you might also find it useful to spend some time, perhaps a Sunday evening, examining your emotional patterns in terms of the six realms. See if you can discover any re-occurring patterns in your behaviour. Next, if there was anyone else associated with the events, look at that person or organisation in terms of the six realms. See if you can determine the patterns of the other individual. Then look at how your patterns interacted with theirs. If you like, add some notes to your journal. See if your new understanding of the realms is insightful in understanding yourself and the behaviour of others.

Once a week, when checking your journal, you can also see if there is something building up that needs to be attended to. If a War of the Realms is brewing, spend some time thinking about it. Determine its nature and causes. Once you have determined that there is an imbalance developing, determine the remedy and apply it. In working with your emotional imbalances, 'The Healing Lights' exercises on pages 129–34 are especially useful.

Another way to overcome an impending imbalance involves paying attention, working with the events that are occurring throughout the day. For example, you may be having difficulty working with a Hell Realm person. Hell Realm people seem to need to be mad at something all the time; they are always looking for a fight and tend to use their anger and rage to force their opinion on other people. In an office environment it is like standing in front of a machine gun on a swivel mount. The gun just keeps firing in circles. Understanding that a Hell Realm person has to be mad at someone or something all the time, and that it doesn't much matter who it is, can help in working with such a person. Because the indiscriminate nature of the anger is recognised, it is easier to take it less personally when it is directed at you. As a result, it won't unfairly influence your decision-making process.

Applying this knowledge is useful in a broader context, too. If you know that your department is about to be reorganised, for instance, you will recognise that the Animal Realm and Half-god Realm individuals will have particularly intense but very different problems that will need to be addressed. Reorganisation causes people in these realms far greater pain and fear than, say, those people who are predominantly Human Realm or Hell Realm. For that matter, major events like reorganisations tend to bring out the Half-god and Animal Realm behaviour in everyone. Knowing this, you can prepare yourself and your colleagues. This is compassion. More importantly, this is skilful compassion.

Working with Emotional Patterns

That truly wonderful thing that started when first learning to pay attention continues to expand and grow when successfully working with emotions. The world becomes increasingly alive. This is the reward for all your hard work. It is gift shared between you and all those around you.

There are two major realisations that result from working with emotional patterns. The first involves the true nature of emotions and emotional patterns and the discovery that there is no one who hasn't suffered some kind of emotional pain. It is a natural part of our experience. We can't avoid experiencing the events that usually give rise to pain, but we can choose how we react to them. By working with our emotional upheavals we can accept the positive and negative events of our lives as a natural part of who we are. We can develop a sense of harmony with our world.

The second realisation is of the true importance of other people in helping us reach emotional maturity. It is abundantly clear that it would not be possible to have the energy, courage or insight to work through so many emotional patterns were it not for work colleagues. Interestingly, it is the people who are most difficult to work with – the mortal enemies in the War of The Realms – who teach us the most. Once you recognise this you will appreciate these people more, and even feel some warmth and empathy towards them. With this comes the ability to treat them more kindly. And when people are treated in this way, they return the feelings . . . and on and on it goes. There is a new emotional chain reaction.

Conflict

When I get pissed off at one of my clients I paint his face on a golf ball. You have no idea how good it makes me feel when I hit that damn ball.
A FORMER EMPLOYER

Never strike to the heart.
THE SEVEN POINTS OF MIND TRAINING

It takes two to tango.
SAYING

Everyone works with people they like – and with people they dislike. We dislike some of them intensely. Seldom is there the luxury of working only with people who are friends or who are in total agreement with us. Given this situation, and because no one particularly likes pain, we tend to be kinder and more attentive to the people we like and to avoid as much as possible the people and situations we don't like. This is what usually keeps people from doing what is fair and/or what is in the best interest of those with whom they share their lives – both friends and enemies.

As we have seen, an increased understanding of mental patterns and greater peace and harmony results in disliked people being treated more compassionately. But it would be a fairy tale to believe that just because people are better treated they will reciprocate. It would be an even greater fairy tale to believe that just because you are becoming a nicer person that suddenly the whole world will reciprocate. It just isn't so. The Dalai Lama was evicted from Tibet; the prisons of the world are full of holy people – some of them imprisoned by other holy people. Nice people don't always win the lottery. It is, simply, impossible to live in the real world and avoid interacting with difficult people. Since conflict cannot be totally eliminated, it is important to learn how to work in a less than perfect world; how to work with people it is not especially enjoyable and/or worthwhile to work with; and how to deal with conflicting wants and needs. The way to start is by taking a look at conflict.

The Essence of Conflict

Conflict arises totally from within. It happens because what is liked is clung to and what is not liked is rejected, be it a belief system, material objects or emotional patterns. Conflict occurs when what is clung to or rejected is in opposition to what someone else is clinging to or rejecting. The magnitude of the conflict depends on how much and to what extent each person defends their position.

Conflict is all around us, on all levels. Even if you have no particular interest in pursuing global peace, and your thoughts don't extend much beyond the end of your driveway, there is still no escape from the problems of conflict. National borders aren't the only places where wars are breaking out; the conference rooms of everyday work lives are stuffed with conflict. So, rather than shy away from conflict, it is better to do something about it.

There are two directions in which to travel. You can work to reduce or change your own wants and/or work to reduce or change the wants of others. Much of what is called diplomacy is based on the latter: changing or reducing the wants of other people. Mediation is the fine art of getting both sides to reduce or change their wants.

Reducing Conflict

Conflict situations tend to be approached from the perspective of the assumed superiority of our own selfish wants, needs, and desires over the assumed secondary importance of the wants, needs and desires of others. If people are skilful in getting their own way, they tend to take on the characteristics of the experienced salesperson pursuing the juicy client account. The experienced salesperson knows that the best way to get his or her own way is to convince the client that what the client wants and what the salesperson wants are really the same thing, even though it usually isn't true.

There is a flaw in this approach. The flaw is this: as skilful as the manipulation of the wants and desires of other people may be, the root causes of conflict nevertheless remain. The clinging and rejecting remain undiminished and unchanged. Such an approach ignores and devalues the inherent worth of the wants, needs and desires of other people.

To do something about this, you need to value other people's needs, wants and desires. You also need to examine your own carefully, to determine what is really important and what is not. Working with emotions and emotional patterns of clinging and rejection is the beginning of this journey. Through working with the exercises in Part 2 you will begin to explore how your patterns of clinging and rejection interact with the patterns of the people around you, particularly the people you work with. You will become aware, painfully perhaps, of how strong your needs, wants and desires are, as are everyone else's. The next step is to observe yourself in conflict situations.

Improving self-knowledge

Begin this process by first taking a look at what you already know about yourself. If you have been keeping a journal, your notes can be of particular use. Spend some time, an evening perhaps, thumbing through your journal looking for instances of conflict in your work and personal environment. Hopefully, you have already spent some time examining both the emotions and the behavioural patterns associated with these events, so there shouldn't be any big surprises.

You now want to see if you can gain an understanding of your patterns of conflict. To do this, pick a single event from your journal which seems to typify your experience of conflict. Read your journal entry. Then spend some time going back in your mind and reliving the experience. At this time, especially if the memory is particularly painful, do the 'Clarifying Blame' exercise on pages 111–114. Try to see the experience as objectively as possible. In particular, try to understand how the conflict started and how it ended. Try to see yourself as well as the other individuals or organisations involved in the conflict as an outside observer might see the episode. If you can, see if you can recognise the patterns that you have repeated in the past and that you are likely to repeat in the future. If you want, write some notes for yourself.

Overcoming Your Own Belief System

As everyone knows, hindsight is 20/20. It would be wonderful if you could apply what you now know to your past. It would be even more wonderful if there were some mystical formula (perhaps in the appendix of this book) which could be looked up and applied to future conflict situations. Unfortunately, there are at least as many reasons for conflict as there are people. Life, fortunately, is not so simply nor so boring that responses can be codified in such a way.

There are, however, some common emotional patterns that run through conflict situations. By beginning to recognise the manifestations of these patterns in your own conflict situations, you can begin to construct the contents of a personal peace plan.

The first of these patterns centres on the relationship between conflict and a personal belief system. Everyone believes in something – even if it's believing in nothing at all. These beliefs are held very strongly. People are quite often willing to fight for what they believe in. Their beliefs are invariably associated with strong emotions such as love and hate – primarily emotions of intense clinging and rejection. They are, in effect, the manifestation of strong emotions as behaviour patterns.

One of the strongest beliefs that is held is the belief in our own permanence and solidity. If your boss laughs at your very best idea for marketing the new line of cough syrup, you feel as if an inch of flesh has been carved from your chest. You are truly, mortally hurt; you are diminished; you are threatened; you fight back for your survival. If your name is mentioned by the Vice President at the quarterly sales meeting, commending your efforts, you grow an extra two inches. You are enhanced; you expand. You will fight for the cause.

Belief systems bring enormous value to a life. They bring a sense of meaning and purpose. But they also carry with them the potential seeds for conflict, since each person's is slightly different. It can be difficult accepting the beliefs of everyone else. People usually want everyone else to share their beliefs. When this is insisted on, however, the seeds for conflict are planted.

Everyone has worked with people with strong beliefs, either in themselves or in some organisation. Everyone has worked with people with lots of strong beliefs; people with opinions on everything from the punishment for taking the last cup of coffee to who should really be in charge of the master production schedule. Strong beliefs are manifested in a variety of ways. Some people love to argue to the death for everything they believe in. Everything has to be a fight. Meetings with such people are sheer agony. Others seem to be in a continual state of suffering over their beliefs. Everything they believe in is being continually threatened. If there is no creamer at the coffee pot, it is a case of personal persecution and the world is thrown into a crisis for days. If someone wants to add an extra field to a report after the computer program is written, it is enough to fuel at least a week of personal suffering.

In each case, someone is right (me) and someone is wrong (you). Someone wins and someone loses. At least one person has defined 'right' and 'wrong' and at least one person has stepped over this self-defined boundary. Conflict is the only 'solution'.

Belief systems are double-edged swords. They can help us focus on the things that are really good in life and avoid getting caught in what is of questionable value. But a belief system can just as easily be detrimental to personal development. Clinging and rejecting prevent people from seeing and doing what is fair and in the best interests of everyone involved.

Focus again on the conflict you singled out earlier and examine it in terms of the beliefs that you held at the time when the conflict occurred. For most people, these beliefs were extremely solid. They probably still are. The design for the new order fulfilment system database was right; the customer service reps can't be allowed to make credit decisions; I knew, I knew, I knew . . . I knew that I was right and they were wrong.

Look at the nature of conflict in the light of your own quest for happiness. Examine your belief system in this light. Take a look at what you believe and why. Also take a look at how your beliefs affect those around you. As you do this evaluation, especially in the light of the suffering which your beliefs bring to you, you may find that some of your beliefs aren't as important as they used to be. You may actually stop believing that you are always right and that everyone else is always wrong. You may also find that the most important beliefs are those that bring people together – not those that divide them.

Surviving the External Pressures

Our business personas are a special form of belief system. They are very real and solid to us and filled with a myriad of preconceptions about what is 'right' and what is 'wrong'. When something occurs – a criticism or a difference of opinion, for example – which contradicts our preconceptions, we immediately react defensively. This defensiveness is the seed of conflict.

To make matters worse, this seed gets planted over and over again. The boss screams at you, so you scream at the first person who walks into your office, and that person in turn goes home and screams at their family. There's a harvest of conflict. If your business persona always has to be right, any attempt to prove otherwise is likely to result in strong resistance. The more attached we are to our beliefs, the more solid and permanent they are, and the more likely we are to be engaged in conflict.

By examining your conflict patterns, you will begin to

recognise that much of the anguish that you have put yourself through could have been avoided by relinquishing some of the solidity of your beliefs. This is not to say that you should now agree with everyone, whatever their opinions are, or that you should accept criticism without comment. Avoiding potential conflict situations, whatever the costs, can be as much an emotional pattern of clinging and rejection as any other. But a difference of opinion does not automatically need to become the grounds for conflict.

Learning to Prevent Conflict

There are three phases in every conflict: the beginning, when the potential for conflict first manifests; the middle, when conflict is in progress; and the end, when conflict is abating. Unless you're talking about invaders from Mars marching up the driveway unannounced, most people can see conflict coming long before it actually arrives. At least it should be possible to see conflict coming, if you're paying attention. The conditions for conflict build over time. Often it's simple, basic likes and dislikes that become the seeds for conflict. So your first task in working with conflict is to pay attention to your likes and dislikes and explore their potential for sparking conflict. You need to be aware that you have likes and dislikes and that they influence what you do, say and think. It is not just your own likes and dislikes that you need to pay attention to. You also need to pay close attention to the preferences of those you work with. There are two tools for accomplishing this. The first is to practice paying attention during daily activities. The second is your morning and evening contemplations. During the day, if you can calm your mind sufficiently, see the play of personalities in your work groups. Pay attention to what makes people happy, what makes people unhappy. In the morning and in the evening you should then be able to observe the impact of these preferences on your own feelings. Are there people who are beginning to irritate you? Is your work style beginning to irritate someone else? Is there someone you are beginning to dread talking to? Is someone avoiding talking to you? Why?

If you can maintain just a small amount of diligence in regard to paying attention and taking time for your daily contemplations, there is much which you can predict about the behaviour of people – who will work well together; who will fight; who will be leaders; who will prefer to be followers. There is a large body of literature and research about personality types and team dynamics to draw upon to support your observations. Without paying attention and your daily contemplations, however, be warned that all the one-day seminars and motivational speeches won't do much good.

Predicting how people will relate to each other is one thing; changing the outcome of situations is quite another. Determining what to do about conflict is the next step.

Determining What To Do About Conflict

The most important thing to bear in mind is that the goal is not to win the war but to avoid the war altogether. One of the unfortunate potential spin-offs from an increased understanding of personality types is that this knowledge can be used to manipulate others. Likewise, through an increased understanding of what people really want and don't want, there is the potential power to use this information to manipulate decision-making. But when it comes to helping people, including yourself, to achieve long-term, true, meaningful happiness, manipulation results in nothing because it only perpetuates the business persona. Rather than manipulating people and situations, it is essential to determine what is truly best for the organisation, and then do whatever is necessary to achieve that. Sometimes that means giving up a lot of personal territory.

To help achieve this, it is necessary to first determine what it is in you that contributes to the conflict situation and make an effort to change it. By working through the Sequential Exercises in Part 2 you will get in touch with yourself on a simpler, yet much deeper, level. One that you don't visit very much. Understanding yourself on these deeper levels is essential to understanding your motivations. Understanding your motivations is essential to giving up your closed, solid, defensive stance.

Overcoming Conflict

You will find that at the beginning of potential conflict situations, you can take advantage of the openness and gentleness you have found during your exercises. You can then use your intellectual spears, the daily contemplations, to help you break through the personal attachments that are contributing to the conflict. At the same time, you can use your openness to help you to tolerate and accommodate the attachments of colleagues.

At the first sign of conflict it is important to determine what in your own personality is contributing to the conflict. Are you being stubborn, condescending or just plain stupid? Most important, are you about to make a stand of some kind, putting yourself on one side or the other of a decision? Analyse the situation in your daily contemplations, and then determine what needs to be worked with. You may find that certain traits need special attention. Intense feelings of anger or frustrated ambition, for example, may need some intensive care. At this time, you might find 'The Healing Lights' (pages 129–34), 'The Outer Elements' (pages 123–9) and 'The Inner Elements' (pages 152–6) especially useful.

It is especially important to get in touch with yourself on a non-verbal level. Your emotional patterns began to form long before you could express yourself in words. Drawing, painting, working with clay, and dancing are all wonderful and useful ways to get in touch with your deepest feelings. Conflict can open the gates to your innermost feelings and become a unique opportunity for self-exploration.

When Conflict Won't Dissolve

There are some times, of course, when conflict simply won't go away, whatever is done. Whether it is an inability on your part to give up an attachment or the inability of someone else to give up theirs, a fight is about to begin. At this time there is a very serious question that needs to be asked: 'Is this something worth fighting for?'

Perhaps on some ultimate, idealistic level there is nothing worth fighting about, but that seems not to be true in this world. For most people there are things worth defending. There are things worth fighting for. The question is, what are they and how can they be recognised?

When a mother sees her young son about to pour the boiling water on the cat, she will grab the kettle. She knows that an argument is likely to ensue, but she also knows that saving the cat is more important than the discomfort of an argument with her son. She knows, too, that allowing her son to abuse the cat will create far more misery for him in the long run than what he is going to experience in the next half hour. Her fight is worth it.

Life is full of boiling water, little boys and cats. When it comes to fighting, however, most people have their priorities strangely aligned. They will fight like tigers to ensure that no one cuts them off in the traffic, but they won't fight for public transport for the less fortunate. They will argue over who gets the commission on the last sale, but they won't do anything to ensure that the client gets what they paid for.

Battles are chosen based on the protection and enhancement of the business persona. The goal is not to see that the team succeeds; only that there is personal success. People fight because they feel threatened. The imaginary persona which they have worked so hard to build is under attack. They fight to protect it.

Is it any wonder, then, that organisations are as unproductive as they are? Energy is totally exhausted in self-protection and self-enhancement; there is little left for the work that needs to be done. There's no energy left for anyone else.

Deciding what to fight for and what not to fight for is an extremely personal decision. It has something to do with words such as 'character' and 'honour'. As you work with yourself, you will find that you naturally, continually, re-examine what is important to you and what is worth fighting for. Is it really essential, after all, to get credit for every success of your department? Is it really essential to make sure that you block the funding for the guy you can't stand in the other department? Do you have to fight over everything? Could you just let things be and accept them as they are, even if you don't come out on top?

Deciding what is important to you and what energy you will put into achieving your goals is central to the maturation of that little child deep inside who is kicking and screaming, demanding its own way. As you work with maturing your true self, not just your business persona, you are on the road to becoming adult.

The Positive Benefits of Conflict

A lot of people really love conflict. It is just about the only time in business life, after all, that anyone can get really emotional. The emotional spectrum that is available, however, is extremely limited. There is a choice between rage well done and rage raw. Conflict is a feeding frenzy for the emotionally starved. They love conflict because it is the only source of nourishment that hasn't been denied. When the wall of the business persona is erected, the supply route to the source of emotional nourishment is cut off. The only thing that seems to get through that wall, in either direction, is rage.

When the rage about this particular situation comes through, so does rage about everything else. This is one of the great dangers of conflict and anger. Not only is there anger about your boss stealing ideas for the new product line, but there is also anger because your previous boss stole an idea. And then there was the time when your older brother . . . . Angry reactions are seldom based on the current situation alone. The unresolved emotions of every event in the past are also waiting for an opportunity to be released. The skeletons are waiting to come out of the closet.

Because they haven't developed an effective means of working with emotions, particularly with the hurtful reactions experienced from past events, everyone walks around with a great deal of emotional baggage. The past hurts are like ugly wounds covered only by thin scabs. Bump on the edge of the table and it hurts a lot more than it needs to because the previous wound wasn't taken care of. Because the emotions experienced in previous conflicts weren't worked through, their pain is bound to be re-experienced. We walk around protecting our old wounds.

So when you're in a conflict situation it is important to recognise that there is a good deal more going on than what is immediately visible. When conflict stirs up intense emotions and patterns of behaviour, the mind uses the opportunity to detect the weaknesses in the persona and shore up your defences. But with a greater degree of self-knowledge it is possible to resist this defensive tendency and instead use the opportunity to revisit past experiences of pain and disappointment and take another shot at working through them.

Everyone has emotional baggage and most of the time it can be hidden away. Conflict, however, is one of the times when it's hard to keep things hidden. You can take advantage of this to get in touch with your buried dissatisfactions and frustrations. Looked at in this way, conflict is not something to be feared. It can be an opportunity to understand yourself better. You do need to prepare for this in advance, however. Your barriers, your psychological rhino skin, must already be soft, flexible and permeable. It is especially important to continue with your daily contemplations during times of conflict, to keep the channels to your emotions open.

Ending Conflict

The way you choose to resolve conflict speaks as much about you as the way a battle is fought. Many people are quite attached to conflict, liking the adrenaline rush, the sense of power – especially if they win. They savour the memory. In some perverse way it makes them feel alive. For others, the experience is quite the opposite. The very thought of another conflict makes them sick to their stomachs. They will do anything rather than go through the experience again. Nothing is worth fighting for ever again. They will stay uninvolved from now on.

Both extremes are just that – extremes. In the first case, the adversary continues to be punished; in the second, it is the self that is punished. Punishment, however, has nothing to do with conflict. At the end of conflict, there is an antidote which should be foremost in the mind – forgiveness. There are two people to forgive: the adversary and yourself.

Forgiving adversaries means dropping the conflict, both physically and mentally. Most people have heard the following Zen story, but it bears repeating. It is the story about the two Zen monks who approach a river. They will need to ford the river on foot. At the river bank there is a young woman who wants to get across but who doesn't want to get her dress wet. She asks the monks to carry her across. One of the monks gets angry and refuses. The second says nothing, picks up the woman and carries her across. As the two monks continue their journey, the first monk who refused to carry the woman continues to fume about the insult. He complains to his companion, 'How could you do that? How could you carry that woman?' The second monk turns to his companion and smiles. 'Are you still carrying her? I put her down back at the river.'

Everyone is carrying young women, young men, two-ton gorillas, elephants and heaven only knows what else on their shoulders. In working with conflict, we must learn when and how to put down the burdens. The burdens are the grudges, bad feelings and resentments that result from conflict – especially when you lose. Conflicts don't end when the last blow is struck. Even before the war is over, the next, bigger, stronger campaign is being plotted.

Conflict takes a lot of energy. A failure to forgive means being locked into a cycle of violence. And like the monk who couldn't put down the young woman in his mind, it means that energy will be expended in keeping the fight going. So conflict is expensive. In a practical sense it means that employees who spend all their time engaged in or plotting wars are not productive employees. They waste not only their time but the time of everyone around them in their personal battles.

Even when you blame yourself completely for it, conflict still takes a lot of energy. Self-blame, guilt and rejection can be equally expensive of energy when pointed inwards. One of the expenses when you blame yourself is the energy put into trying to make things right again. There has been a mistake and things need fixing, but even with superglue they will never be the same. Rather than going forwards, a great deal of time is spent trying to fix the past. Trying to make things right again implies an unwillingness to accept your own fallibility and the fallibility of others. It is difficult to acknowledge that mistakes have been made.

The sadness of conflict is that everyone has to live with its outcome. Conflict changes relationships. This has to be accepted. It is essential to the process of forgiveness. There are two techniques in particular that you can use after a conflict to help regain your emotional balance, forgive yourself and your adversaries, and get on with your life.

The first is a contemplation that you can do in the evening, or some other time when you want to work with it. Its theme is very simple and it goes like this: we all want to be happy, each and everyone of us. What has just happened between ourselves and someone else is because of this. We wanted to be happy. Each of us, in our own way, tried to do what we thought was necessary to be happy.

If you feel now that it was you who was misguided, then you should try to feel some satisfaction that you had an opportunity to learn something which you didn't know about yourself. Perhaps now you have a better understanding of what makes you happy and what doesn't. You should ask yourself, 'Is this something that I could have learned some other way? Is this maybe the only way that I could have learned this lesson?'

The same can be said of the lessons that your adversaries have learned. Even though they may have experienced a great deal of pain, was this best for them in the long run? Was it best for everyone involved?

If you can, make your thoughts towards others kind thoughts, based on the remembrance of your own struggles and the pain. Conflict is a shared experience of pain. Use it as an opportunity to develop your empathy for others.

When conflict is not positively resolved for everyone concerned, your feelings should be those of regret and compassion. Your adversary may not have learned valuable lessons; perhaps you have not learned lessons as well. In this case, you are both likely to repeat the same patterns of misery over and over again. It is not a very happy thought. Not something to rejoice about.

There are two meditative exercises described in Part 2 to help further this transformation of your mental and emotional patterns. 'The Friend' (pages 141–3) and 'Universal Compassion' (pages 157–60) will help you to get in touch with your feelings of forgiveness and compassion on a deeper level.

Improving Productivity

Some time in the next week or so take a walk. Walk down the corridors of your own organisation. Imagine what it would be like if there was no one there but you to do all the work. Imagine all the skills and experiences sitting in those chairs, standing at those work benches.

For every person you alienate, you create an obstacle for yourself and your organisation. Whether that person falls out of the workforce and you absorb the cost in unemployment fees or they join the competition and your company absorbs the cost in reduced margins, everyone pays.

To be productive, everyone needs to work together, all heading in the same direction. No one can succeed if the rest of the team fails. Learning to work effectively with conflict is the single most important thing that can be done to improve the productivity of organisations.

As well as improving organisational profitability, there can also be an enormous gain in personal productivity. There can be differences of opinion without wars. People can feel free to share their ideas with you because they know they will not be rejected when they don't agree. By letting down the walls, a little light and fresh air comes in.

Competition: Winning and Losing

Why do you always root for the underdog?
KHENPO KARTHAR RINPOCHE

Winning isn't everything – it's the only thing.
AMERICAN FOOTBALL COACH

Business is about competition. It's about winning and losing. Or at least that's what everyone tells each other. If your business isn't successful, the mortgage doesn't get paid and the kids don't get fed. The message is: 'If you don't compete, you don't survive.'

The world we live in is full of competition. We live in frightening times, when many countries seem determined to beat their neighbours into oblivion. It is a world, all things considered, which it is very tempting to withdraw from. It's tempting to try to make a killing on the stock market and then retreat to a place in the country. If you don't have the patience or skill for that, then it's tempting to look for a reasonably soft job with a good retirement plan and hold your breath until you're sixty-five.

But think what would happen if all the 'good guys' in the world were to say, 'I don't want to be bothered; it's just not worth it,' and remove themselves from the heat of political and economic competition. What would become of the rest of us? There are more than enough people who like being bothered (provided there is something in it for them) and are eager to step in and start making our decisions for us. Those decisions are not likely to be in our best interests, however.

When thinking of the word 'compassion' many people think of a rather gentle form of behaviour rather than warriors or competition. But if compassion is considered in its broadest sense, it may be that the kindest, most compassionate thing that can be done is to strive as hard as possible to provide a safe and harmonious environment in which to live and nurture spiritual development.

Creating a compassionate society takes more than kind thoughts and good intentions. You must learn to compete on the same field with everyone else. You must learn to compete against those people and organisations who do not share your interests and who are planning a very different world. As much as you might want to, it won't work to abdicate your social responsibility and retreat to a cave, country cottage or mountain cabin and think happy thoughts. Instead, your compassion must be tough. It must be fearless. You must learn how to compete. You must learn how to win – and how to lose.

The first and most important lesson you need to learn is when competition is worthwhile. The overwhelming majority of the competition which people are currently involved in is totally unnecessary and detrimental to their physical, emotional and spiritual health – not to mention the physical, emotional and spiritual health of those around them. This is because people are competing in the wrong ways and for the wrong reasons, and when they do 'succeed', their goals are achieved in the wrong way.

For the majority of people it is impossible to talk about competition without also talking about conflict: the two are synonymous. This is where the problem with competition begins, for it is a misconception that competition and conflict stand side by side. To compete in a healthy, constructive way, the concepts must be separated. Healthy competition – winning and losing – has nothing to do with conflict – anger and aggression. Instead, it is about achieving our maximum potential for compassion and kindness. Competition facilitates the good we want to achieve at work and in the world.

This is, of course, starting to sound familiar. 'Unlock your true potential', 'Achieve your maximum success' . . . These are phrases that everyone has heard before. This is where most self-improvement plans begin. But beware: there is a great danger in approaching self-improvement by first learning how to compete. The danger is this: learning to compete without understanding your own patterns of aggression is likely simply to further entrench those patterns. The result is dissatisfaction masked beneath the guise of 'success'. This 'pseudo success' actually makes it more difficult to acknowledge the dissatisfaction that results from the gap between the inner self and the business persona. It numbs the pain. It is like treating the gangrened leg with heroin and continuing to walk.

Competition involves active engagement with the world around us, and this has a direct and profound impact on the people we work with. It is the externalisation of our inner desires, habits and emotional patterns. As such, it is something that should be thought about very carefully. Before seriously engaging in competition, it is wise to at least have a working knowledge of your inner desires, habits and emotional patterns. A successful approach to competition requires not only a willingness but also the skills to take responsibility for our actions and their outcomes, regardless of what they are. It requires maturity and stability of mind.

Fortunately, your work on yourself – your efforts to understand yourself better and your efforts to learn how to work with other people in difficult circumstances – is preparing you in just this way. You are ready to consider competition. This does not mean, however, that you should now expect to be the best at everything you attempt, or that at times you may not fail abjectly. That would not be realistic. What it does mean, is that you are ready to be successful at the *process* of competition. You are ready to engage in competition without worrying unduly about hurting yourself or others.

The Dynamics of Competition

Competition is one way that we respond to the less than compassionate goals of others who do not share our altruistic ambitions. In these situations we tend to think of only one thing –

survival. But there is more to it, for healthy competition can be far more than just a defence mechanism. Here is a quick look at what happens when people compete, starting with you.

In your evening contemplations, examine your own competitive behaviour. Do you play golf or tennis? Are you trying to become a director? Win an especially lucrative sales account? If you like, go back to your journal and examine your thoughts at a competitive time. The questions you should ask yourself are, 'How did I behave at the time?' 'What were my thoughts, especially towards other people?'

Like most people, when you look back at how you competed you may well see a lot of rough edges. Did you cheat? Did you wait for your opponents to make a mistake and then jump for joy when they did? Did your animal instincts come out? Did you trample on the feelings of people around you? How did your behaviour change from what it is when you are on holiday, say? Which person do you prefer?

When competing, people push themselves, they stretch themselves. They test limits – theirs and their environment's. They take risks. As a result, they often feel both physical and emotional discomfort. Competition forces them to work outside their habits. It irritates them. It makes them itchy and scratchy. They work very hard when they would rather be on the couch watching television. They make sacrifices of short-term gratification so that greater goals can be achieved in the future. They also compare themselves against a measure – whether they want to or not. They open themselves up for scrutiny, relinquish privacy, ask someone to tell them if they are good or bad.

Competition does a wonderful thing – it creates cracks in the veneer of our projections. We're a little less civilised when we compete. Mainly because we are directing less energy towards keeping them up, our barriers come down. For a time there is an opportunity for communication with our inner selves. Not only do our inner feelings have an opportunity to express themselves but we also have an opportunity to observe how we really are. It may not be a pretty sight but it should be interesting.

Healthy versus Unhealthy Competition

When we are competing in an unhealthy way, our goal is to enhance our business persona, to puff ourselves up, to feel big, to make other people feel small. But if our attitude is healthy, competition becomes an opportunity to strip away the layers of projection, to become small, to break away from being mindlessly locked in behaviour patterns.

As you examine the patterns of your competitive behaviour in your evening contemplations, try making an inventory of your most recent competitive efforts. Were they healthy or unhealthy? Did they build the walls or tear them down? Your inventory may well reveal far more unhealthy than heathy competition. This may be a distressing revelation – especially if you have spent time opening yourself up a little in the contemplative exercises. It would not be difficult to become discouraged and give up on competition altogether, seeing it as a destructive force. Equally, it would be easy to aim at mediocrity and diminished goals, simply because it no longer looks possible to win. For most people, at some time in their lives, that is exactly what they do; for one reason or another, they give up. But giving up your dreams in the hope that will make you happy is not the answer either. Resignation to fate is not the same as happiness. Cowards aren't happy.

Unfortunately there are no quick fixes. As you work with yourself, you must be patient. You will improve slowly, sometimes in ways so small they are barely noticeable. Your competitive behaviour – how you go about getting what you want – will reflect the healthiness or unhealthiness of your mental attitudes more than anything else that you do. The emotional process of competition will show you to what extent you are directly experiencing the world around you in colour, not shades of grey; how happy you are. As you learn to compete correctly, as you learn to try hard for whatever is important to you, your attitudes will gradually change. You will mature step by step. If viewed in the right way, if prepared for correctly, competition can be a very quick path to getting to know your inner self and then changing it for the better.

Seeing Competition Differently

Most people recognise three components of competition: themselves (the heroes), their opponents (the villains), and the game itself (the holy war). Each is seen as distinct and separate. But, in fact, these distinctions are an illusion. Opponents can take many forms. They can be external: other people or organisations. But they can be internal as well: me against my tendency for laziness; me against my lack of organisation; me against my fat cells.

When people compete, they build artificial barriers between themselves and their opponent. Far more to the point, they identify their opponent as an obstacle standing between themselves and the goal that they want to achieve. They are competing because they want something which they think will increase their happiness. It is only one more logical step to deduce that if the opponent were to go away, they could be happy. And just another step to deduce that it is their opponent's fault – just for standing there – that they are unhappy. It is not hard to come to the conclusion, then, that if they are to be happy – to win – then someone or something else must lose. This is why competition is almost always accompanied by conflict.

To overcome such feelings, the competitors must go back to the very beginning. They should return to the basic split which they think exists between them. This was their first mistake. In creating this separation, they failed to recognise and value the interdependency between all the components. It was somehow thought that they could win the game playing on a field by themselves without a ball. Buddhists have a beautiful term for this interdependency. They call it 'the Threefold Purity'. What it means is that you (the subject of the action), your opponent (the object of the action), and the action itself are inseparable. The separation is an illusion.

What that means to competitors, especially in a business sense, is that they fail to see the competitors and the competitive environment as actually a part of themselves. Furthermore, they fail to see competition as integral to their personal and professional growth. They think that happiness is more likely if the competition goes away. They think they would be happier if the work week were ten hours long. They think their competitors and the competitive situation are the cause of their problems. In fact, they are their redemption.

Recognising and appreciating this interdependency is the key to eliminating conflict and other destructive emotional patterns from competition. If the competitors, opponents and the competition itself are inseparably bound up together, personal success cannot be separated from the process. The opponents are not standing between the competitors and their happiness; they are their opportunity to achieve that happiness. As such, it makes far more sense to treat them with respect and appreciation than with animosity. This is, of course, much easier to say than do.

Today it is fashionable to talk about win-win situations. Every business proposal mentions the concept at least once every ten pages. 'Partnership' is another buzzword. It is also popular to talk of problems as 'opportunities'. Perhaps this new language is the part that is actually right in business.

It may be possible to understand win-win intellectually by seeing problems as opportunities, but there is no mechanism in place for an emotional understanding. The result is that it is fairly easy to sell win-win (but not more than once to the same customer), but it is virtually impossible to deliver. How many projects, after all, actually finish with everyone happy? How many reorganisations don't upset someone – or everyone?

Learning to Let Go of Dualism

Non-adversarial relationships really are good business. But it is difficult to apply this consistently and over the long term. To achieve real win-win results in competition, you have to appreciate non-duality – that the idea of separation is an illusion. Grasping this concept requires more than an intellectual process. You have begun this journey already with your morning and evening contemplations. Just as you draw in a deep breath and exhale slowly, for just that moment you can let go of 'me' and 'them', you can let go of duality. (Without an in-breath there can be no out-breath – and vice versa.) The thoughts of 'me' and 'them' may return in a heartbeat, but for just that moment, as you gaze out of the window or into space, you can let go. It may not seem like much, but it is a start, a very important start.

Repeat this experience throughout the day, at any time. If you are paying attention, pause for that moment, draw in a deep breath, exhale, and recall that experience of harmony, of non-duality.

To deepen and broaden your appreciation of non-duality, continue with the exercises in Part 2. As you work through them, there is not too much that should be said about their results. It is best to do the exercises without too many expectations or preconceptions. It is best to see and judge for yourself. But there does seem to be a direct correlation between a relaxed mind and a mind free from intense, dualistic emotional patterns. A relaxed mind is less likely to be a hateful or a jealous mind. A relaxed mind is far better prepared for competition, since it can perform at its best.

Facing the Results of Competition

A healthy attitude towards competition requires a healthy attitude towards the outcomes of competition – winning and losing. Again, Buddhists have a beautiful phrase that sums up their attitude towards winning and losing – 'equal taste'. 'Equal taste' means that whether they win or lose, the experience is valued equally. Winning and losing taste the same.

Winning and losing are relative terms. The same activity performed in two different environments may have two drastically different results. A product line which may be 'world-class' in a protectionist environment may rank as a third-rate copycat in an open market. Winning and losing depend entirely on who is being competed against. But if you let your happiness be determined simply by who shows up to compete, you are handing over responsibility for your happiness to the whims of fate. If you want to be truly happy, you must dissociate your happiness from the measuring-stick of others.

This may sound like encouraging you to be indifferent to the outcomes of competition. But it isn't. Anyone who has ever been part of a winning experience, who has felt the pure elation of doing their very best and being the best, knows that it would be depressing to give up that kind of experience. The point of equal taste is not to feel indifferent to winning and losing. It means learning to accept the pain of losing and to value it equally with the joy of winning.

Once again, it is the daily exercises and contemplations that teach you not to be afraid of the intensity of your joy and pain. You know now that you can deal with them, whatever their nature. Knowing this, you can develop a certain fearlessness with regard to the goals you set for yourself. You know that you may crash – but you needn't burn.

Test your preparedness in your contemplations. Do this on an evening or weekend when you have some extra time, perhaps as much as two hours. Begin by trying to recall a time when you failed abjectly at something that you really wanted. Perhaps a job that you were passed over for or an award that went to someone else. If you have journal entries for that time, go back and read through them. Try to get in touch with how you were feeling at the time. Try to get in touch with the disappointment, the pain. Most people's tendency, especially if they were particularly hurt, will be to shy away from such memories, to avoid thinking about them. But resist the temptation. Especially if you are the kind of person who relives your glory days over and over, it is important to relive your inglorious days too. It is important to acknowledge both parts of your experiences.

Now you can work with the secondary emotions that invariably accompany disappointment. Try to recall how you behaved in the hours, days and weeks that followed. Try to recall how you felt and how you made other people feel. Did you pout? Did you look for excuses, blame someone or something? If there was blame or guilt associated with the occurrence, you may want to do the 'Clarifying Blame' exercise (see pages 111–4), and perhaps some writing or drawing too. Try to clarify any lingering pain or disturbing emotions, such as resentment or bitterness.

Examining secondary behaviour – resulting from how you feel about winning and losing – is very important. It is the manifestation of either rejecting the pain of failure or coveting the joy of success, and it communicates a great deal about who you really are.

The amount of time this process takes will vary depending on how much you need, or want, to work through. Take enough time to come to terms with the experience because, as you have probably already discovered, your previous experiences of competition are having a direct impact on your present and future experiences. Understanding the past helps you to understand the present and future.

On a different evening, but soon after, repeat the exercise. This time look for an occurrence in your life when you were successful. Recall how you felt. The joy. The satisfaction. Then again, work with your secondary emotions and actions. How did you behave after winning? Were you arrogant, aloof?

This exercise does not need to be done very often, perhaps no more than once or twice a year. After completing it for the first time you may find that you only need to repeat it a few months after each new competitive experience, after the results are in and you have had time to observe your behaviour. You can then make a comparison between your behaviour during the most recent competitive experience and previous experiences. You can measure yourself and determine by your own standards if you are improving or not.

Losing does not have to be a negative experience. With a little ingenuity and some ancient wisdom from Atisha and *The Seven Points of Mind Training* it is possible to turn deficiencies to advantage. Losing, for instance, is an especially powerful opportunity to develop compassion. Always remember that when anyone loses, they hurt. So by using the technique of turning adversity into advantage, use your own experience of losing as an opportunity to develop empathy for the suffering of others. It is then possible to look differently at all those people who have been labelled as losers. Losing, if viewed in the right way, can be a powerful mechanism for transforming your self-understanding into understanding and appreciation of others.

Winning, too, can be every bit as much of an opportunity for developing compassion. Winning provides the opportunity to experience joy and it is this same joy that should be desired for everyone else. In the midst of the tedium of the work day, it is all too easy to forget this joy. Winning is a reminder of just how good it can feel. The challenge is to sustain it and to share it.

By taking your personal experiences – which are at their most intense during competition – and transforming them, you become kinder, gentler and more sensitive. If looked at in this way, it really doesn't matter if you win or lose. Either way you win.

Working in a Team

In today's business environment, competition takes on a special challenge for management. That challenge is called team-building. Today's businesses are big. Very big. They span continents, cultures, languages. When people compete, they do so through massive projects. Little in business these days can be achieved by solo performers. Virtually all of today's great achievements are the result of teams of people, all working together towards a common goal. Designing a car, implementing a global computer system, building a telecommunications system, all require countless numbers of people pooling their talents and efforts. No single man, woman or child can stand up and say 'I did it. All by myself, I did it.'

In this environment everyone needs to learn to compete not as solitary heroes, but rather as members of finely tuned teams, all pointing in the same direction. Managers need to learn how to build and sustain these teams. This means that they need to learn to work co-operatively and with trust. Empathy for the individual challenges of those around can help build such an environment.

There is much talk and effort in business these days centred around the deployment of teams on large-scale projects. Teams are at the heart of the quality movement. Innumerable psychologists have made small fortunes analysing and building models for how teams work. There is a lot that can be learnt from this work, but you also now know that the approach to working with personal winning and losing works especially well in group environments.

COMPETITION: WINNING AND LOSING

The special challenge of working in teams, however, is that individuals have to modify their way of working to blend in with the rest of the team's work habits. This is seldom easy. Many people find working in teams an exceedingly uncomfortable experience. For it to work, you have to pay attention not only to the competitive goals of the team but also to the competitive goals of the individuals within the team. There can be a big difference between the two, and this is where many people and their teams fall down. The team experience fails because people mistakenly equate success in the team environment with individual excellence rather than organizational excellence. This results in confusion about how and when to compete. Consequently, a great deal of time is spent competing against each other rather than directing energy towards the team goals.

We all compete all the time – for affection, attention, power or praise – whether we're aware of it or not. Difficulties in teams arise from the fact that this competitiveness is not sufficiently acknowledged and channelled outward, rather than inward against our team-mates and ourselves.

Using the technique of paying attention it is possible to maintain an awareness of your own self-destruction and cannibalistic competitive behaviour in a team. There are several remedies to help you deal with this. The best answer, of course, is the mental maturity that comes from working steadily through the Sequential Exercises in Part 2. This is the bedrock on which everything should be based. In addition, use the 'Working with Intense Emotions' exercise on pages 109–11. Be careful not to neglect your daily journal, and reserve extra time for painting, walks in the park and whatever else helps you to stay relaxed and calm.

It may be tempting to set grandiose objectives for yourself in a team environment. Everyone wants to be the superstar of team relationships. But your objective as you work in a team environment, especially at first, should be far more humble. For your first goal, learn how to not let your own obnoxious, misdirected competitiveness interfere with the objectives of the team. Don't make a nuisance or an obstacle of yourself. By now, you should be able to tell quite clearly when you are doing just that and adapt your behaviour accordingly. Accomplishing this will be a monumental contribution towards the harmony and success of any team that you work on.

Second, there is the challenge of dealing with the competitiveness of your team-mates when it is actually directed towards you. You can, of course, choose to sit for the umpteen months in weekly meetings with your teeth clenched and endure. Apart from dental work, you will survive. But, based on what you already know about yourself, you can do more. You can turn adverse conditions into advantages, using your irritation, anger, frustration and every other imaginable emotional response as opportunities to let go of those very things in yourself which are being irritated, frustrated and bothered.

When people are irritating or frustrating, it is because they are touching something in you, quite often painfully. They get through the veneer of your business persona, they get under your skin. In your quest to build a bigger and better business persona, you shore up your defences as much as possible to ensure they never get through again. You build your walls higher, thicker, stronger. Now is the time to abandon that practice: dismantle your business persona and use all the attacks to help you with the dismantling process. Every time someone irritates, offends or makes you angry, use the occasion to remind yourself that you affect other people in exactly the same way. The causes may be different, but you still frustrate and irritate people, just the way they frustrate and irritate you. Remind yourself of how they must feel. You can then use that memory to explore your own actions and determine what needs to be modified or improved. In effect, turn every situation inside out: use what happens as a reminder of what you do to other people and what you can reasonably expect them to do in return. Use phase two of 'The Mirror' exercise on pages 136–8 to help you.

You are not just changing your business persona here; not just putting on a smile while continuing to seethe with anger just under the surface. Instead, you are working directly with the anger itself. You are also working directly with the jealous, lazy, selfish and all the other destructive components of your personality that are so counter-productive to success. Now you can and should expect more from yourself. You have the means to develop the emotional and mental maturity to be able to make and stick to these decisions. You need not be driven by your own wants, needs and desires; you can choose your goals, rather than being driven to them and by them.

Limits

Don't put the horse's load on the pony.
THE SEVEN POINTS OF MIND TRAINING

Do the most difficult things first.
DR AKONG TULKU RINPOCHE

Working with the exercises in Part 2 to develop a greater sense of self can have its problems from time to time as you test yourself more and more. You might get discouraged or worried about your results – or lack thereof. But be assured that nothing will be fatal, and however slow and awkward your progress there will be some overall improvement. There is nothing that can be said, thought or done that will be so messed up that it can't be corrected. With this understanding you can feel comfortable and secure doing the contemplations and exercises, knowing that even if you don't do them quite right or quite often enough, there is always a way to correct problems and get back on track again. It might even allow you to feel secure enough to take a few chances.

Inevitably, there will be times when you will run into problems, and come up against your own limitations. Sometimes you may find that when you are doing the exercises, no matter how letter-correct you may be, you can detect no beneficial results. For long, long periods of time you may experience no joy despite all your efforts; indeed, your personal life may seem to get worse, not better. It seems as if nothing is being accomplished. The process isn't delivering. Alternatively, it may be difficult to get down to doing the exercises; you are practising them inconsistently or out of sequence; it is difficult to finish them; instead of paying attention you find that you are walking on eggshells. It seems that the process is impossible to work with.

It would be an extraordinary person who didn't suffer any of these setbacks. The process which is being engaged in is not a weekend's work, not even a week's. It is a life's work. Over the course of the months, years, even decades, a fair number of missteps should be expected. Self-work is a messy, messy business. Fortunately, there are remedies that can be applied.

Special Remedies

These are a collection of contemplations, exercises and techniques that can be applied to correct certain problems as you progress along this path of self-work. In some cases, the special remedies will be the same exercises that have already been done – but perhaps applied in a different way or for a different duration, or maybe even in a different location. In other cases, they will be unique to the problem that they are designed to correct.

All of these special remedies – whether they are directed towards problems with the process or problems with the results – begin in the same way: identifying the problem in need of a special remedy. To do this, the same techniques that are already being used are applied, this time to examine the well-being of the process itself. Contemplations and journal entries give clues to where you are coming off the track. From time to time as you are doing your contemplations, stop for a moment and check your progress towards taking control of your life. How are you feeling? Are you happier, more relaxed, more in harmony with your environment? And how are other people feeling about you? Do they trust you more, do they respect you, like you?

Most people live in a world of business. This means they live in a world that demands results. They have budgets, production quotas, project deadlines to meet. Their performance is measured. There is nothing 'soft and fuzzy' about these demands.

Companies need to make a profit; employees need to be profitable. With something like 'feelings', however, it is much more difficult to define success or failure. How is happiness measured? What are the Personal Key Performance Indicators (PKPIs) for happiness? And, most important, how can self-work be quantitively determined when related to professional productivity?

While it is hardly a precise science, there are ways in which this can be done with reasonable accuracy. In examining your results, you should be looking for a slow, gradual improvement. Nothing dramatic; nothing earth-shattering. Just the kinds of improvements that happen to people who practise a task correctly on a regular basis. Do not be overly concerned with day-to-day occurrences or ups and downs. One bad day does not disqualify the entire process. One complaint or negative comment from a colleague is no reason to panic. What you are looking for is trends. What have the comments been like over the last six months? What has your inner turmoil been like?

This is important to remember. For while you should not be unduly concerned with the opinions of other people – your happiness is your own responsibility, remember – their opinions should not be entirely ignored. If seen in perspective, the opinions of other people can be an extremely useful barometer of progress. If everyone you are working with is angry with you all the time, then this may be an indicator of trouble; if everyone is praising your work all the time, then perhaps you are doing something right.

This applies to feelings as well. While there is no need to be particularly concerned with the minute-by-minute ups and downs of your daily emotional dramas, you should be concerned with the trends. In general, are you happier, more relaxed? Or are you always angry, always paranoid? Do the cycles of your emotional upheavals have fewer dramatic peaks and valleys? Or are you still on an emotional roller coaster? How do you really feel?

In taking stock you might find it useful to establish your own set of Personal Key Performance Indicators. Then, as you continue with the contemplations and exercises, even if very badly, you will soon discover that you have a few 'hot spots'. You will discover at least one – and probably far more – areas in which your own limitations are hindering your ability to work effectively both on your own and with other people. Perhaps you will discover that you are always defensive when new ideas are presented; perhaps this is keeping you from ever having the opportunity to lead a project team or to be successful in delivering innovative results. Perhaps you are totally oblivious to the feelings of the people around you; perhaps this has resulted in your being blind-sided time and time again with complaints, rebellions and unanticipated resignations.

Whatever they may be, use these deficiencies to your advantage by using them as a yardstick against which to measure your improvements. This is where your journal is so especially helpful. It is a living record of progress. From time to time go back to your journal and review its contents to see whether you are improving or just going sideways. Select one or two of your PKPIs and pay special attention to recording your daily relationship to them over a period of time, and you will have a powerful review process.

Stress

One of the most useful PKPIs that can be monitored is the level of stress which you are experiencing. Increased levels of stress are one of the key indicators of being off track.

Everyone is familiar with stress whether it's from their own experiences or from media coverage. Learning to cope with stress is critical as it is present each and every day. Many of the contemplations and exercises in this book are targeted specifically towards relieving the experiences of stress. Sometimes, however, the process itself can cause stress. For instance, if you become totally involved in doing the exercises, an element of the Leather Road Project can creep in. Look for indications in your journal and contemplations that this is occurring. It isn't hard (provided you are paying attention, of course) to identify when your efforts to improve yourself are contributing to your stress, rather than reducing it. If the joy and pleasure disappear completely from doing the exercises, especially for an extended period of time, you can be pretty sure that you have got a problem.

The problem may well be related to working with other people, especially 'difficult' people. Although hard work, doing these practices should not be stressful on your working relationships. Nor should they be a burden on other people. Team dynamics should improve. If, however, in learning to pay attention you find that you are distancing yourself, or holding yourself aloof, especially from the people you find it most difficult to relate to, then this is a problem.

If this is the case, don't feel unduly bad – or mad – about it. Everyone has their limits and just by embarking on these exercises you are going to start coming up against yours. Stress will undoubtedly feature among these limitations precisely because it is one of our most common reactions to experiencing our limits. As such, stress is not likely to go away soon. You are unlikely to wake up one morning perfectly generous, open, compassionate, brave and honest – and totally relaxed and at ease with yourself. You will experience your limits as long as the gap between your inner and professional selves exists.

But the extreme manifestations of stress – anxiety, tension, fatigue – place their own limits on the work you are trying to accomplish. Extreme stress makes it especially difficult to recognise and work with the root causes of stress, making you your own worst enemy. It is difficult to take the corrective measures, namely the contemplations and exercises, which are the antidote. The result is that extreme stress leaves you with little, if any, way to resolve or at least make peace with your limits. You are stuck.

To overcome this stage, you need to work on deep relaxation. This, above all else, relieves the pain of stress. Only when the pain is at a manageable level can the rest of the contemplations and exercises do their work. The most effective way to do this is to go on a relaxation retreat.

The Relaxation Retreat

The relaxation retreat is a collection of special remedies packaged in a particularly effective, intense format. There are several qualities that make a relaxation retreat well suited for dealing with the extreme discomforts of stress. One is removal from the source of the stress. A retreat means just that, getting away, and a required ingredient of a successful retreat is separating yourself from those things that are triggering the stress.

A cabin in the woods can be a wonderful break from the hectic nature of work, as long as you leave behind your cell phone, computer, modem and pile of paperwork. Likewise, it is essential to leave behind all your mental baggage. Walking in the woods, head down, planning next week's presentation, isn't going to help relaxation.

Some people can turn off their professional minds fairly easy by refusing to answer the phone, sitting back in their favourite chair and, well . . . relaxing. For the majority, however, the solution requires a lot of planning.

The first task in preparing for a relaxation retreat is to determine what venue is really the best place. Should the retreat be at home, or should it be somewhere else? If going away, perhaps to a cabin or a hotel, should the retreat be alone or would a managed group be more helpful? If going alone, your self-discipline needs to be good so that a schedule of contemplations and exercises can be devised and followed through. Likewise, if going alone it helps if you know what to do on a retreat. Do you have a clear idea of what is the most effective way to attain deep relaxation? Or could you use a little expert advice? Do you just need to unwind a little or are you in need of some major help? While there's no absolute answer, generally the more stressed out or wound up you are, the more you should seriously consider the support of a managed group retreat led by a trained facilitator. When in doubt, opt for company.

Managed group retreats also provide another advantage which is worth seriously thinking about – access to individuals who are doing the same self-work. If you have been doing your self-work alone – perhaps you have been working entirely from this book – then access to fellow travellers may be a real plus. So, too, may be the interaction that a group retreat provides. If you are exploring how you work in groups, trying to improve on your levels of co-operation and/or leadership, then a managed group retreat provides an invaluable means to explore these relationships.

Whether you choose to do your retreat at home or away; whether you choose to do it alone or in a group, the deciding factor should always be how can you achieve the deepest relaxation in the quickest, safest way possible? There is a network of organisations supporting managed retreats (see page 164). They are under the direct supervision of Dr Akong Tulku Rinpoche, are especially trained to help you get the most out of a relaxation retreat and have completed the contemplations and exercises described here.

In a managed group retreat, a schedule is provided – which helps, especially if you haven't been on one before. But if you are doing a retreat alone or with an informal group, some planning is required. In part, this depends on how long the retreat lasts. It would be nice to think it could be possible to get away from work for a month or two to relax. But that hardly seems realistic or practical: you are more likely to have a long weekend. Try and aim to take such a retreat two to four times a year, three to six months apart. If you can, a one- to two-week retreat once a year, substituted for one of the three-day retreats, is even better.

Planning a Retreat

The goal is to achieve deep relaxation in a relatively short period of time. To do this, it is essential to emphasize the special remedies targeted at relaxation. These should be exercises designed to help the body and mind relax; exercises designed to help self-expression in non-verbal ways and (especially) exercises designed to provide for mental relaxation.

Massage

For physical relaxation, the key is completely non-competitive, non-aggressive physical activity that enhances feelings of 'connection' to the physical body. There are a variety of activities that meet this definition. Casual walks, yoga and t'ai chi can each serve the purpose. Your attitude towards physical activity is important as completion should not leave you too tired. It should also take a minimum of mental exertion. Ideally, it should be possible to let your mind flow freely while the physical activity occurs. That is why competition is out.

There is one other aspect of physical relaxation that should be included in a retreat – touch. It's a sad reality of 'civilised' society that people no longer touch each other unless it's sexual. The nurturing touch is sadly limited. There is strong medical evidence indicating that touch is beneficial, however. Studies show how petting an affectionate animal can soothe elderly people in nursing homes or calm someone ready for surgery. Equally, a loving touch is critical to the life of newborn babies, especially premature ones. Somehow, however, those people who are not so near the thresholds of life are forgotten about. On a retreat, the therapeutic qualities of touch can be explored through massage. The retreat should include at least one, probably two, sessions.

The people giving massage don't have to be trained: anyone can rub another person's feet, hands or back. In a group retreat setting it is possible to spend some time exchanging gentle hand, foot and back massages without any risk of hurting someone. Massage is no big deal.

You don't necessarily need anyone else to massage you either. Admittedly, there are parts of the body that can't be reached, but most people can grab their own toes and fingers. You can massage your hands and feet and give yourself a neck-rub. So even on a solitary retreat, you can include massage as part of your programme.

The key message when massaging either yourself or someone else is kindness. Massage is a simple, straightforward way to be kind to another person – or to yourself. For some people, the thought of massage, especially in a group setting, remains nothing less than terrifying. It's just so incredibly personal. The thought of giving a back rub to the guy in the next office stirs up any number of confusing images. Most people can far more comfortably consider massage from a complete stranger than from someone they work with. Especially in this age of sexual harassment suits, people in professional environments simply don't touch – ever. Hand, foot and back massage, especially on a structured group retreat, can be a safe yet powerful lesson in both giving and receiving simple kindnesses.

Non-verbal Expression

Most people don't think too much about how they express themselves. They talk, write, and 'verbalise' in a variety of ways. But long before we could express emotions in words, back when we were babies and young children, we had other ways to express our feelings. One of those was 'art' – painting, sometimes with fingers; working with clay; using glue, paper and scissors; drawing with crayons. Sometimes we threw paint; sometimes we drew on walls. But somewhere along the road to adulthood, all the colours and pictures were left behind. Our first mode of communicating was lost. Only a few people kept on with the paints and the clays; for the majority only one mode of expression is used – words.

There are things, however, that can't be said in words; there are feelings to get in touch with that can't be reached with sentences. This is frustrating, whether it is realised or not, and the best way of overcoming the problem is by returning to earlier modes of expression. On a retreat there should be two to three sessions playing with colours and shapes. The idea is not to think of 'art', but to put feelings down on paper or shape them in clay. The emphasis should be on expression. Paint anger if that is the feeling; or paint unhappiness. Or try another way: if angry, maybe paint peace; if unhappy, maybe paint something joyful. Be creative. One of the ways to ensure that play doesn't get too serious is to use big, sloppy tools. For painting, choose poster paints or acrylics – nothing delicate or subtle. Use big brushes or maybe fingers. Have fun. Make a mess.

If you are on a group retreat, managed or otherwise, it can be possible to try doing shared paintings and artwork. Working in pairs or as a group, create collages or murals – anything that requires sharing the same art mediums with others. This provides a powerful, yet simple, way to explore group dynamics. It is possible to find out a lot about how you work with other people by watching how you go about painting a mural with five or six others – and without saying a single word.

Mental Relaxation

These are the same exercises that have been done on a daily basis. If you are part of a managed group retreat, your group facilitator will select the exercises and may even add an exercise or two which will be similar to, but not exactly like, ones that you are already doing. Otherwise, you should make a selection of the exercises that have given you the most relaxation. Try to do a mixture of exercises that you have already been doing and new exercises that are coming up soon in your schedule. A retreat is an especially effective way to begin the Sequential Exercises in Part 2. Attending a managed group retreat is a good way to find out exactly how the exercises are done and to get some advice and encouragement along the way.

In an informal group, it is best to take turns leading the exercises. (If the group is managed, a facilitator will do this.) People who participate in group retreats invariably mention that one of the most pleasant and powerful experiences that they have is having someone lead the group through the exercises. The leader should speak softly and evenly, first describing the exercise, and then letting it unfold over time. They need to give enough silent space between each instruction to let the participants fully experience each phase. They should also 'remind' the group periodically of what they might be feeling or of the next step in the exercise. Again, this should be done in a soft, even tone of voice. Finally, the leader who is keeping track of the time, talks the group through the conclusion of the exercise.

Mixing the Special Remedies

A mixture of approximately 25–30 per cent non-verbal communication activities, 25–30 per cent physical activities and 40–50 per cent mental relaxation exercises is the best combination. Do a little of each type of activity each day, distributing them evenly throughout the time available in two- to three-hour segments. The exact sequencing isn't incredibly important. Common sense will dictate the fine tuning. For instance, don't plan massage or a relaxation exercise involving lying motionless on the floor for immediately after a meal.

Food and De-toxing

A retreat should be relaxing for bodies as well as minds, so it would be as well to give the body a break from hard-to-digest foods like animal proteins and heavily processed foods. But be careful, too, on the other side of the equation. If you are unaccustomed to vegetarian meals, especially legumes and grains, this may not be the best time for double servings of nut pâté with tofu sauce. Generally, the lighter the food – soups, salads, fruits – the more comfortable you will feel. Retreat, too, is a wonderful opportunity for a little de-tox – giving your body a break by taking a rest from alcohol, caffeine and nicotine.

To provide a flavour for what a retreat might be like, and to help in planning one, a sample schedule tailored for deep relaxation is included in this book on pages 162–4. This schedule can be used for a solitary retreat or in a group setting.

Other Times to Use the Special Remedies

You don't have to wait for a retreat opportunity before you can apply special remedies, especially for stress. All of the remedies that can be done on retreat can also be done at any time whenever a little special help is needed. Perhaps you can take some time off on a Saturday afternoon and go for a walk, or turn off the television some evening and get out your paints and brushes. Perhaps on your next business trip you can go for a walk in the evening rather than sitting in the hotel room contemplating the mini-bar.

All of this requires, of course, that you recognise when such remedies are needed. The best of medicine makes no difference if you never take it – or if you take it only after you are almost dead. Medicine is most effective if it is taken before the illness causes too much damage to the body. The same is true for the special remedies. They work best if they are applied before your nervous breakdown takes hold.

The best way to see that this happens is to have regular check-ups using your evening contemplations and journal. From time to time, you should reflect on how you are doing, perhaps thumbing back through your journal looking for patterns. When you find that stress levels are on the increase, you should do something about it. Right now.

Support Groups

There is one other very important way in which you can ensure that you take your medicine on a regular basis and this is through support groups. All the special remedies that are practised on retreat can also be done in a support group environment in your home town, perhaps even at your office. Working in informal groups you can establish a schedule of 'meetings' every week or two where you get together, paint a little, throw clay, take turns leading the relaxation exercises, do a little hand, foot and back massage, and in general enjoy each other's company.

If you decide that a support group could be helpful to you, there are a few things to keep in mind to ensure that it's successful. The first is keep it simple. Your group doesn't have to have officers, a newsletter, a series of public events, or board meetings; it doesn't have to do anything but get together as friends and share each other's company and practise the special remedies.

Nor does your group have to become an emotional crutch for one or more members. It is not intended to be traditional group therapy. While there's nothing wrong with a little commiseration, meetings are not the time for mutual psychoanalysis. Instead support groups are a powerful way to maintain contact with individuals who are sharing the same personal journey. They are the equivalent of fellow travellers, banded together for support, inspiration, encouragement and maybe just a good laugh or two. In this time of networking, they are your network of contacts to help you get where you want to go as quickly and as safely as possible.

If this seems like something that might interest you, there is some start-up help available. The same organisations who provide retreats, listed on page 164, can also give you information about other individuals in your area who are interested in support groups.

Making Progress

Stress is, of course, not the only reason for doing a retreat, joining a support group, or applying special remedies. There are as many things that can go wrong with the process of doing contemplations and exercises as there are people doing them. Everyone has the capacity to get it wrong in their own unique way. And everyone has the capacity to correct it – also in their own particular way.

It's extremely important to understand this. The self-work that you are doing is based on the belief that you are capable of working through your own problems. No one is going to knock on your office door and say, 'Hey, you're getting stressed out. Let me fix it for you.' It is something that ultimately you have to do for yourself. Even if you take advantage of every retreat, every support group, even seminar, and read every book, it is still yours to do. Only you can make yourself happy.

How you go about tackling the problems you encounter is a great indicator of your personal progress. The ways in which you work with your limits – how you detect them, adjust to them, use them as opportunities for growth – can be one of your most powerful PKPIs. At first, your efforts are likely to be rather clumsy and heavy-handed. You will find that you won't recognise your limits until they slap you in the face. You won't recognise that you are consumed with rage until you blow up at your best friend or your boss. You won't recognise that you are suffering from extreme stress until you realise that you haven't had a good night's sleep for weeks.

Later, as your self-work matures, you will be able to recognise when you are getting in trouble and take corrective action before you get too far out of balance. You will learn how to maintain your balance rather than continuing the cycle of falling down, dusting yourself off, and then getting up again. Instead, perhaps you will only wobble a bit, make a minor adjustment, and then continue. With this growing understanding comes the ability to make better choices about what you can reasonably hope to accomplish and what is better left to another time. As you understand more about your limits you will discover that you are able to live within their bounds, managing them rather than being swept away each time you encounter one of them.

Even more importantly, you will come to understand that each time you hit one of your limits, you have an opportunity to learn something. There are no negative experiences, only negative reactions to them. This is an extraordinarily exciting thought. For what it means is that you can make peace with yourself – while at the same time striving for improvement. At last, you can start dropping your business persona. You can cross the gap between who you are and who you pretend to be. It's OK for everyone to know that you have flaws. Let's face it, they know about them anyway. It was only yourself you managed to hide them from.

You can witness your own transformation. You can acknowledge the help of good friends, the guidance of a centuries-old tradition, maybe even good timing – but ultimately you have the satisfaction of knowing that you did it by yourself. Furthermore, you can undertake the even larger risk of transforming yourself into who you really want to be. You do not even need to be afraid to take chances; you do not need to fear that you may fail. Whatever happens, there will always be a remedy; there will always be a path forward.

One of the most important lessons you will eventually learn is that it is difficult to live gracefully with your limits. At some point in your personal progress, you will come upon the crushing realisation that you are not who you pretend to be. This can be exceedingly difficult to take – gracefully or otherwise. But learning to live gracefully within your limits is important. It involves a balanced mix of your present condition – mistakes and all – and striving for an improved future. This attitude, more than anything else, will help through the rough times when you can only see your limits and nothing seems to be working. The benefits of this attitude in your working life are enormous. Close your eyes and imagine what working for such a person would be like. Imagine working for someone who is at peace with themselves, who knows their own strengths and weaknesses, and who doesn't try to be anything but what they are. Imagine what it would be like to have your team feel the same way about you.

Riding the Tiger

When the mind is still, guard it as a mother guards the sleep of her infant child; when the mind is restless, herd it as the elephant-herder leads his herd of elephants.

OCEAN OF CERTAINTY, VITH GYALWA KARMAPA

A Bodhisattva (a realised being) never worries about his reputation.

THE SEVEN POINTS OF MIND TRAINING

A poor man doesn't have to worry about his will. He doesn't need a lawyer; he doesn't need to worry about who will inherit his wealth, he doesn't need to worry about whether his ungrateful in-laws will use his money wisely or squander it. He is too busy worrying about the problem of just staying alive to consider the world around him.

Once you were poor, dirt poor. You were a mental and emotional pauper. But you are no longer poor. You are very, very rich. Once, the only thing you could think about was your own predicament. But things have changed. You have changed. You have changed how you view the world; you have changed how you interact with the world.

And like the poor man who suddenly finds himself with a winning lottery ticket, you need to decide what you will do next. Suddenly there are choices, possibilities which could only be dreamed of before.

The changes that are occurring will have left you in a rather unique situation. You are not like everyone else because you are beginning to know who you are. You know your strengths and your weaknesses. Yet you are exactly like everyone else because you recognise that you hurt and feel, laugh and cry just like everyone else. There is nothing that makes you special. In business and in the rest of life this gives you an enormous advantage. The ability to identify what you do well and to do it, while at the same time identifying what you don't do so well and finding someone else to do it, can give an appreciable advantage.

But, like a teenager with their first driver's licence, your newly earned powers have their own unique responsibilities. You might be tempted to squander them. You will be surprised however to discover that the exercises in this book are difficult to exploit. This doesn't mean that they are without power – indeed, there is an enormous strength here, more than can ever be imagined. It simply means that this path can't be easily used in the ways that are usually associated with power: personal aggrandisement and control. Instead, you will find that personal happiness isn't about 'me, me, me'. Nor is good business. Personal happiness and good, successful business are possible only when the chant is changed to 'us, us, us'. Now you can do that. You have the strength; you have the wisdom.

Making Your Choice

Are you now content with the level of personal happiness and professional competence you have achieved so far – or do you want to stretch yourself, do you want to constantly explore new ways to work with yourself and others? Now that you have tamed the tiger, do you choose to ride her? And if so, for how long, and for how far and how fast?

For each person this will be an extremely personal decision. As the exercises designed to work with emotional turmoil begin to bear fruit, your individual needs will become less intense. It will be easy to relax. It will be easy to say this is good enough. But remember that while you may be changing, the world around isn't. More than ever, it is a dark and dangerous place. And there are a lot of people suffering. As you go through life, as you go about your daily business, pay attention to the world around you, to the wash of emotions, the passions, the despairs. They are all there, every day, all the time. Those people are you.

The need in today's world for people who are willing and capable of riding the tiger, who thrive on riding the tiger, cannot be overestimated. In business, the need for clear-minded, rational, individuals willing and able to put their own egos aside to work collectively towards complex solutions is more important than ever.

Business is at a crossroads. Local economies are becoming national economies; national economies are becoming global. The lines between corporations and national governments are becoming increasingly blurred. More and more, organisations are looking to global technology solutions, to standardisation across continents and cultures. The problems are so complex that no single individual can have all the answers. More than ever, the success of teams will affect the success of business.

But it is working in teams that is the single most difficult task to be encountered in business. It requires that the boundaries between personal territories be flexible and porous. Working in teams relies on compromise and co-operation. It requires that personal agendas are put aside in favour of the organisation's agenda. The organisations that succeed will be those that work most effectively as teams. Everyone has the same technology, so the only thing that differentiates them is the people. What is necessary is a workforce of sane, well-trained (and continually retrained), mature-minded individuals. The challenge for companies is to find these people and to make sure that they are kept happy. If they can't be found, they will need to be grown from within the organisation.

Transforming the Workforce

The essence of enlightened, compassionate management, is the creation and maintenance of a work environment that not only supports and nurtures those workers who are already sane and mature-minded, but also functions as a greenhouse in which embryonic kindness, sincerity and basic decency can be allowed to grow and blossom. The companies who can provide this environment and successfully transform already existing workforces into these 'superior' people are the companies who will succeed. The managers who can lead and champion these efforts will be the heroes. This is what it means to ride the tiger.

Heroes have many interesting qualities. One of the foremost is a hero's ability to cope with personal fear. The difference between a fool and a hero is that the hero knows exactly what he's getting into; he's absolutely terrified. A fool doesn't have a clue what the risks are. Business doesn't need fools; business needs heroes, armed and prepared to deal with fears and risks.

By far the greatest fear in business today is the fear of change. The world, especially the world of business, is changing very rapidly. Entire categories of jobs are disappearing and technology is changing in quantum leaps. Someone entering the workforce today no longer expects to stay with the same company, or even the same career path, for an entire lifetime the way their fathers did. The only security a worker has is the knowledge and skill he or she carries. Those who survive and thrive will be those who are able to cope with change. This requires that people know who they are, that they define themselves not in terms of who they work for and what they do, but rather based on something deeper, more internal. Their challenge is to guide organisations through change and a manager in touch with his or her inner self will be able to help others do this.

It is strange to hear words like 'compassion', 'hero' and 'wisdom' spoken about in business. They are not usually the terms that are first thought of, especially during Wednesday-morning staff meetings. But this is indeed where you can be heroic. In showing and expressing compassion for others, it is you who will be treated the kindest of all. Over time, your vision and motivation will gradually shift from your own problems to the problems of others. In Buddhist terms, and perhaps in the terms of several other traditions, you begin to develop selflessness.

If you can't quite make the leap to accepting altruism as the best, most self-centred way to be kind to yourself, then consider the alternatives. What happens if you don't guide your organisations through change? What happens if you don't help them?

What happens if you abandon your fellow-workers to their fears? What happens if fear overcomes them?

Cults prey on fear. When people are afraid, they look to anything that offers guaranteed safety. Cults, above all else, offer the promise of security, the security of belonging to something that will never abandon them. In essence, they offer protection from change. A cult is nothing more than a group of people who have lost their inner centres; surrendering themselves to something or someone else who can act as a surrogate for what they lack. This spiritual fatigue manifests itself in any number of ways. Whether it is via fanatical religious beliefs, political beliefs, racial or tribal beliefs, authority and happiness are surrendered to someone else.

It is the same with business. In many ways, businesses are run like cults, preying on people's need to belong. The lives of employees are surrendered to an employer who makes them feel safe. If they are afraid of change, people surrender to the first organisation or individual who can hold change at bay. Employers use this fear to drive productivity. People will do anything if you give them the illusion of security.

This is the risk that everyone runs. But ultimately it is up to you to choose the businesses that you will work for and own. There is no one else to turn to. If you don't reach out and help the people around you, then they will turn somewhere else, anywhere else. If you want to work for and own businesses that you can be proud of, then take responsibility to ensure that those businesses are created and thrive.

In the Buddhist tradition there is the concept of Buddha activity. Buddha activity is essentially the knowledge and capacity to do exactly the right thing at the right time. Totally appropriate action. This is where you are heading. This is where the tiger is taking you.

In the long run, it doesn't really make any difference which tradition you follow. It doesn't matter if you choose the approach presented here – or some other that is better suited to you. What does matter, what matters desperately, is that you do something. If you don't, then you have no one to blame but yourself. You will get the world that you deserve.

PART 2

The Exercises

In this part of the book, Venerable Akong Tulku Rinpoche has gathered together a series of mental and physical exercises aimed at helping you understand and tame your own mind. The exercises are based on traditions and experiential knowledge that goes back for centuries, but Rinpoche has brought the exercises forward into the modern world, tailoring them to modern lifestyles. In particular, these exercises have been selected for their effectiveness in helping people to cope with the challenges they face when working in groups in offices and factories.

The exercises originate in the Buddhist tradition, but they are not 'Buddhist' *per se*. They should certainly not be considered to be a commitment to Buddhism or to any other religion. They have been specifically designed to make them accessible to people from any religious tradition – or none at all. They seem to belong to some larger spiritual tradition that transcends the common boundaries between what are called religions. You may find, however, that from time to time something strikes a harmonious chord with your own religious beliefs. Rinpoche has often said that one of the benefits of these exercises is that they can strengthen your spiritual ties to whatever religious tradition you already belong to. So, if you find yourself 'translating' the exercises into your own religious iconography, it's quite all right.

The importance of doing the exercises cannot be overstated. Reading the first part of this book without doing at least some of the following exercises could be compared to watching an exercise video while sitting on the couch munching potato crisps. It might be entertaining but it won't do much to change the shape of your body – or in this case, the shape of your mind. You may argue that there isn't time in the your day for another single thing, but the following exercises will help you to get back your mind and consequently get back your time. What you 'lose' in exercise time will be 'gained' in personal productivity and overall quality of life.

There are two sets of exercises; the first set is done daily over the course of approximately two years – or indefinitely if you so choose. They take approximately 30 minutes most days, longer one or two days a week: 15 minutes in the morning and 15–25 minutes in the evening. Put them in the same category as brushing your teeth and taking a shower. This is your mental hygiene programme. This section also includes a couple of 'first-aid' exercises, to be used whenever you need to deal with emotional turmoil.

The second set of exercises is a progressive series of activities that more or less follow the chapters in the first part of the book. The entire series takes approximately two years to complete, working at a pace of about 30 minutes a day, six times a week. How long it actually takes will depend on you and your schedule. A schedule (with the duration of each exercise) is suggested on pages 115–7. Follow it or devise your own, but always work through the exercises in sequence. You should also work on each exercise until you 'understand' it. This may take longer than the indicated time.

A second way of using these exercises is to use them as part of what can be called 'Applying the Remedy'. Once you have completed an exercise as part of the sequence, you can come back to it at any time and apply it to your current situation. For example, if after doing your evening contemplations and your journal writing you discover that you are growing increasingly frustrated with a situation that you can't resolve then you can do the 'Red Light' exercise (see page 132–3) for a few days to restore your emotional balance.

No one pretends that this is going to be easy. Taking the time to do morning and evening contemplations, keeping a journal and doing the daily exercises is going to be a challenge. It may be hard sometimes to see the benefit. You may have a tendency to procrastinate. But time will not make your present situation any better. The longer you procrastinate, the longer you'll be stuck on the Leather Road Project. At these times, keep in mind what the meditation master told the young female practitioner. The meditation master was giving a commentary and instructions on the preparation for the time of death. The young student interrupted and asked, 'What if I just think about my guru at the time of death. Won't that be good enough?' The meditation master's reply was swift. 'It would be much better,' he responded, 'if you would do what your guru taught you.'

Location, location, location . . .

Before beginning to do the exercises, give some thought to where and when you will be doing them. In general, the critical success factor is solitude. You will need to find a quiet place where you can be reasonably guaranteed not to be interrupted. This can be at home, the office, or somewhere in between. Given the nature of today's business schedules, you are likely to need to be creative and resourceful in finding your 'quiet times'. The Daily Exercises can be accommodated in an informal setting but the Sequential Exercises, due to the concentration which they require, need a more structured location.

Solitude can have many definitions. It doesn't necessarily have to mean physical isolation. If you travel for your work, for example, either locally or beyond, you can find some creative time on your journeys to do the Daily Exercises. If you fly, a seat in the terminal between flights looking out of a window into the distance can be quite wonderful for the daily exercises. So can a flight itself. If you drive as part of your job, you can pull the car off to a scenic vista and stare out of the window while you do the exercises. When you're not travelling, get in to the office a little early – or stay a little late. Find a window and do the exercises standing or sitting while staring into space. If you get caught most people will assume that you are just being reflective, not a bad thing for people to think of you. If you enjoy outdoor sports such as golf, fishing or water sports, a few moments sitting at the edge of the lake or looking out over the fairway as you practise 'Doing Nothing' can be enormously relaxing.

Alternatively, of course, you can do the exercises at home or in your hotel room. The key component is to find a quiet place where you can be reasonably assured of being left alone and where your surroundings don't unduly remind you of things to do. (Staring over a cluttered desk or into a cluttered room tends to create too many feelings of guilt and too many 'organisational' thoughts.)

For the Sequential Exercises you will want more privacy than an airport or the office cafeteria. For these, you will definitely either need a space at home or quiet time at the hotel. If you're at home, try to reserve a part of the house for at least an hour each night – even if you don't use all that time. There's no need to make a big deal of what you're doing. It doesn't have to take up that much space, nor do you need mausoleum silence. 'Shut up, kids! Mummy's meditating!' really doesn't need to be a sentence spoken in your house. Nor are your exercises a sufficient excuse to get out of doing the dishes.

It's likely, especially with the way that business is going these days, that you will have to be flexible and creative in how you schedule your time as well. The important thing, however, is that you do schedule your time. The exercises have been purposely tailored for short periods of time to fit into 'crazy' schedules. Everyone, even you, can find 15 minutes at the beginning of a day and 15 minutes at the end of a day. If you can't, then this in itself is an indication of the insanity. Find the time. Use it. Every day.

Posture

The way people hold their bodies is truly interesting. Everyone can mentally conjure various stances associated with one or another set of human qualities. Head high, chest out, for example, conveys a sense of bravery and courage; on the other hand, a head bent down with slumped shoulders communicates defeat or humility.

Think for a moment about yourself and the journey you are about to begin. Words like 'dignity', 'self-respect', 'confidence' are useful to keep in mind. When you do the exercises in this book, your body posture should reflect your attitude towards yourself. It is amazing what a straight back can do for a person's self-confidence. Your posture, whether sitting, standing or lying prone, should reflect the importance that you place on what you are doing and the respect which you feel for yourself and the exercises. If you keep this in mind, whether you have paused to look out over the meadow at the end of a two-mile run or you are lying on the floor behind the desk at home, you will be able to find the right posture.

When thinking of meditation or meditative exercises, most people conjure up images of ascetic-looking individuals sitting on hard cushions with their legs knotted in ways the Western body is generally no longer capable of. But this need not be the case. As you approach these exercises – or any other relaxation exercises that you might want to do – think about how you are going to position your body. All of the exercises can be done sitting; some can be done standing; others lying prone. The instructions for each exercise include recommendations for postures.

Even though you need to be flexible, there is no need to throw out 2,000 years of wisdom regarding body postures. The traditional sitting posture recommends sitting with legs crossed, back straight, bottom slightly elevated on a cushion, hands palm down on knees, and head tipped slightly forwards. If you can feel comfortable sitting this way, there are several benefits. According to traditional wisdom, the mind is calmer when the limbs of the body are drawn up close to the body rather than spread out (for example, sprawled on a couch). Additionally, if you want to learn how to do exercises for longer periods of time, then learning how to sit cross-legged will be useful.

Exercises can also be done sitting on a chair. In this case, the feet are placed flat on the floor. (Take high heels off.) Place your hands simply, palms down, on the top of your thighs; keep your back and neck straight. Either look out of a window or down towards the floor a few feet in front of you.

Some exercises can also be done standing up. For these, stand with your feet a foot or two apart, your knees slightly locked and your hands at your sides, clasped in front of you, or behind your back. Either look out of a window or down towards the floor a few feet in front of you.

Some exercises need to be done lying down, in which case lie on your back on a soft mat or a carpeted floor. Depending on the condition of your back and the rest of your body you may need support cushions under your knees and possibly your head and the small of your back. Your arms should be at the side of your body. Your palms can be up or down. Don't fold your hands across your chest and don't cross your ankles.

A final point needs to be made about keeping your eyes open or closed. Unless otherwise stated in the instructions, the exercises should be done with your eyes open, preferably staring out into space. There are several reasons for this. First, doing the exercises with your eyes open places the exercises within the context of normal work life, in a sense making them a more natural part of a daily routine. If you can learn to do the exercises with your eyes open you will find it easier to slip into one in whatever environment you are part of. Second, if you have trouble staying awake, then doing the exercises with eyes open is also helpful to avoid falling asleep, especially when doing the relaxation exercises.

Having said all this, the 'when', 'where' and 'how' of your exercises comes down to common sense. Everyone considers themselves to be professionals with an understanding of how to do good work. That same sense of professionalism and hard work should be applied to your life. The exercises are every bit as important as any other single thing that you do with your life. Keep this in mind and you will succeed – whatever the circumstances.

The Daily Exercises

Commit yourself to doing these exercises on a regular basis for at least two years. After that, if you find them useful, you may want to continue indefinitely.

The key to success is consistency. A little bit every day is much, much better than a whole lot every once in a while. Apart from the content of the exercises, you are also setting up a pattern of self-care and of paying attention to yourself. You need to take care of yourself every day, not just when you are feeling sick.

Doing Nothing

Timing: 10–15 minutes.

Posture: Standing up, seated in a chair or seated with your legs crossed, preferably looking out of a window. Your eyes should be open.

Sometime between when your eyes first open in the morning and when you first start answering the phone and/or making calls, spend 10–15 minutes Doing Nothing. Do this every morning; Doing Nothing is even more important than eating breakfast.

Find a time and place where you can be certain of being uninterrupted for ten minutes or so – it really won't take much longer than this. Put your feet up on the desk, and sip a cup of coffee if you like. Most importantly, make sure that you won't be seen, heard or interrupted. If there is a window available, pull your chair up so that you can look out at the sky comfortably. Or find a relatively uncluttered wall and gently direct your attention to it.

Begin by doing relaxed breathing – five breaths, held slightly on the in-breath. Each time you breathe out, preferably through your mouth, send all your thoughts, your entire 'to do' list, outward into space where they dissolve. On the in-breath, breathe in freshness, vitality, a sense of freedom. Repeat this cycle five times. (For more details, see the 'Breathing' exercise, pages 117–8.)

If you feel any calming in your mental activity, then hold this sensation as long as you can, just looking out into space with a clear mind. As your thoughts gradually return, let them. But rather than getting caught up in the mental activity, try to envision them as clouds moving across the horizon. There's no need to do anything about them, just let them drift past. Let them come, let them go. Let them be.

As your thoughts begin to return, become aware of your surroundings, the chair, the view out of the window. Try to 'see' without making judgements or having opinions. Just 'be' with your surroundings. Treat your thoughts in the same way.

Next, turn your 'seeing' to your own body. How are you feeling? Tired, restless, tense, sluggish, energetic? Pay attention to any physical conditions which may affect how you will behave today. Repeat the 'seeing' with your mental condition. How are you feeling mentally?

At this point, 'judge' your physical and mental condition without placing any guilt or blame or praise. If you are feeling any discomfort or if you feel out of balance in any way, send the imbalances into space with your out-breath. Sense that they are evaporating just like early morning dew.

End the session when you have a sense of balance and harmony. If you like, do your daily planning at this time. Try to carry this awareness with you for as long as you can.

Doing Nothing Too

Timing: 10–15 minutes.

Posture: As for 'Doing Nothing'.

Do this exercise after the primary work of the day is done. Try not to wait until too late in the evening before beginning. A good time is generally immediately before or after dinner. In that way you will be more relaxed to enjoy the rest of the evening.

Begin the session as you do in the morning – with relaxed breathing. Again, observe your surroundings and your feelings, both physical and mental. This time, however, pay more attention to how you feel about the people who you have been working with today. Pay particular attention to the beginnings of negative emotions such as resentment, impatience, anger, or jealousy. Also pay attention to numbness or indifference. What are you ignoring?

If you are working with a particular chapter of this book or a certain exercise, you can also use this time to contemplate how it applies to your own experiences. End the session by taking note of anything which may need some extra work.

Keeping a Journal

Timing: 5–10 minutes.

Posture: Sitting comfortably at a desk.

Keep a daily journal, preferably writing it in the evening. If you can, try to do this immediately after your second session of 'Doing Nothing'. On average, making your journal entry need take only five or ten minutes. This is not a literary work and jotting down notes and phrases is quite sufficient. Write just enough to capture your thoughts in such a way that when you look at an entry later you will recall the events and feelings being described.

When you first start keeping a journal, concentrate on recording your feelings and always make certain to do the 'Doing Nothing' exercise before beginning. Are you happy, sad, stressed-out, frustrated? In particular, note unresolved or frustrated events: an incorrect impression that someone has of your work; a difference of opinion that you can't resolve; broken promises; a feeling of distrust for someone. Look too at 'positive' events: friendships; the excitement of shared ideas; romance; praise from your boss; work well done. Anything, either good or bad, that wakes up your conscience or your emotions. Note, too, anything that you should have reacted to, but didn't. Perhaps situations where you couldn't get in touch with your feelings or where someone has accused you of indifference. Get to know yourself, your patterns. Later, as you work with the chapters in Part 1 of this book, you can begin to work with the feelings you are experiencing, especially as they relate to other people.

Each day give the day a score: a plus if it was a good day; a minus if not so good; a zero if neutral. Devise your own numerical scoring scheme. You can make it as complex or simple as you like. Once a week you can review the week. A quiet evening at the weekend will be best. This will probably take as long as half an hour, so leave yourself some extra time. Review the past week's scores and events. If you want to, revise scores – but don't erase the original score. Then add up the total to score the week. Reflect on your results. At this time, particularly if you see some re-occurring patterns, you might find it useful to do one of the 'first-aid' exercises – either 'Working with Intense Emotions' (pages 109–111) or 'Clarifying Blame' (pages 111–4).

Every so often, repeat this process, this time reviewing the prior months. How has the year been going, the last quarter? This will obviously take a bit longer to do, but if you have kept up with your journal it won't be too difficult. This is a useful activity to do in the evening during a relaxation retreat. It may even propel you to do a relaxation retreat.

Basically, your journal is your record of who you are and who you are becoming. It is for you alone. So be as honest as you possibly can. As you work with your journal and with the contemplative exercises, don't be surprised if a lot of 'junk' starts coming to the surface. You may start remembering feelings that you have had buried in your subconscious for a very long time. You may also begin to have an increased awareness of the feelings that you are having right now.

At times these feelings can be intense. The following two exercises, 'Working With Intense Emotions' and 'Clarifying Blame', are designed for those times when you need to 'work through' something or simply cope with an overwhelming emotional onslaught.

Working with Intense Emotions

Timing: 30–60 minutes.

Posture: Find a quiet and safe place where you can look out into the sky without being interrupted. This may be standing on a hilltop, sitting on the bank of a river, or even sitting in front of an open window.

This exercise is designed to help you deal with intense emotional turmoil, the type of turmoil which won't let go of you but keeps on pulling you back to a particular pain. The first task, of course, is to recognise that you are indeed in the midst of such turmoil. Your journal should be helping you with this. So too should your daily paying attention. As soon as you recognise that you are absorbed in this type of intense emotion you should find time to do this exercise: don't wait until you are in complete emotional collapse before you begin the healing process.

Begin the exercise by trying to empty your mind of thoughts. Practise the 'Doing Nothing' exercise, spending more time on the breathing portion, breathing in deeply, pausing on the in-breath, then exhaling strongly. Repeat this until you can feel your (racing) heartbeat slowing down slightly. If you possibly can, try to find a moment's peace.

Then, just let your emotional pain rise to the surface. Let go of each thought or emotion that comes to the surface. Peel off the layers of emotion, just like the skin of an onion, one layer at a time. With each layer, send it off into the space in front of you, letting it lift gently and then dissolve. Pay particular attention to the dissolution of something that was dark, heavy and solid to you. See the emotions as nothing more than dark smoke.

There will be tens, hundreds, of layers of emotions. Continue sending them all into space. Let go of them, letting them lift from your shoulders and your chest. Eventually you should begin to feel some lightness, at least some sense of ease from the enormous burden that you are carrying. When this occurs, turn your attention to your emotions. Start out by asking yourself, 'What is this emotion?' This may seem silly at first, but think about it. What colour is your emotion? Where is it? Is it in your head, your heart? Your big toe? What does it taste like? Look like? Close your eyes if you like. Try to find exactly where this emotion is in your body. Try to find its centre. Get as close to it as you can. Embrace it. As soon as you find the centre, go to the centre's centre, and so on. Continue until you are at the tiniest point, the atom at the core of your emotion. And then beyond. To nothingness.

When you have found this centre, or this core of nothingness, or when you can at least imagine it, open your eyes and look out into space again. Take a deep breath or two. Now imagine all these layers of emotion, all the layers surrounding the centre, floating away into space one after another, dissolving into nothingness. Let go of the emotion. Feel its emptiness, its insubstantiality. Sense how transparent it is.

For a few moments, you should feel a lessening of your emotional intensity. Let yourself experience this in just the way that you let yourself experience your emotional turmoil.

Eventually, perhaps in a few minutes, perhaps longer, your emotion will become solid again. When this occurs, repeat the exercise, again dissolving the emotion to nothingness and sending out your feeling, seeing it dissolving into space as the lightest of thin tissues. Repeat this cycle two or three times - sometimes it may take more – until you feel some emotional calm and that you have integrated the experience into your life in a healthy way. This may take as little as half an hour, or as long as an hour.

At some time during the cycles, you may want to ask yourself, 'Where is this emotion coming from?' If the emotion is the result of an experience with another person, perhaps an argument with a colleague or a loss of some kind, then ask yourself, 'Did this person cause this emotion? Really? Did they put it inside me? Are they to blame?' If this emotion is the result of your own failings, either real or imaginary, then ask yourself, 'What created this emotion? Where did it really come from?'

If your feelings of emotional pain are accompanied by a sense of blame, either towards yourself or someone else, then it is important to resolve this blame. Try to remember, try to feel what is common to everyone – everyone wants to be happy. For whatever reason, this event occurred because someone wanted to be happy. If you can, perhaps after you have been working with this exercise for a few days, maybe even a few weeks or months, recognise the mistakes of the event which has caused your pain. If they were your own actions, then recognise your mistakes, forgive yourself – and go forward. If it was someone else's mistake or negativity, try to understand the reasons for the resulting action.

Of course, intense emotions aren't going to go away in a single session. You may feel some relief for a while, but soon the emotions will come rushing back again. Depending on the depth and intensity of the emotion, you may need to repeat the sessions for days, weeks, even months. As you continue working with yourself, remember to make notes in your journal. As you progress, from time to time return to your journal and review the earlier entries. It may be helpful to observe how your emotions change as you work with them.

Clarifying Blame

Timing: Unquantifiable.

Posture: Sitting comfortably.

Especially if the feelings are related to a personal experience associated with a great deal of pain, there may also be a great deal of blaming going on. Where there is pain, especially in

Western society, there is usually blame. In our minds, the pain is due to the failure of someone or something to meet our expectations. Placing blame is a lot like the scar tissue on a wound. It can be smooth and in time completely disappear; it can also be dark, and permanently disfiguring. This exercise is like plastic surgery for our souls.

There are two types of situation where this exercise can be useful. The first is as you recognise that you are placing blame in a current situation. Here timing is important. The sooner you can begin this exercise, the sooner the healing process can begin.

The second situation is somewhat more complex. Doing the exercises in this book is likely to stir up old memories, some of them extremely painful. Memories of broken relationships, deaths, or intense embarrassments can stir up feelings for decades after their occurrence. As these recollections occur you have an opportunity to heal the unresolved emotions that remain.

In both cases, the process is the same. It begins by recognising you are blaming. The blame may be directed towards someone or something else, or towards yourself. You should continue doing this exercise from time to time until you reach a point when the memory of the experience no longer brings with it an emotional reaction. You will know when that time occurs. For extremely intense experiences, don't be surprised if this process continues over several years, maybe even decades.

You will need paper and pen and you may also want some art materials such as paints or clay. The exercise contains three steps. You can do these steps in the same session or in separate sessions, but they need to be performed relatively close together in time.

Begin by doing a relaxation exercise, perhaps 'Working with Intense Emotions'. Then write down your experience of the blaming situation. Tell the story from your own perspective. Explain what happened, explain the injury to you, explain how you felt at the time, and how you feel now. Try to actually re-experience the event. If you like, use your journal to record some notes. After you feel that you have remembered the entire event, examine your feelings towards it. Try to identify your emotions, and in particular try to identify your feelings towards other people and external events. This can result in a lot of writing, or just some brief notes. When you have finished, read what you have written back to yourself. If you like, go for a walk or take a break for a cup of tea. Give yourself some time to reflect on your feelings. Perhaps you could create a drawing or make something in clay.

Now repeat the exercise. This time, however, write the event from the perspective of your adversary. If you are blaming yourself, put yourself in the shoes of your victim(s). Try to experience the event with their feelings and their thoughts. Try to understand how they were feeling. Again, when you are finished you may want to take a walk, have that cup of tea. If you want, you can also work with paints and clay, again from the perspective of your adversary.

Finally, repeat the exercise from the point of view of a neutral bystander. Someone who has no vested interest in the experience. Try to see the event from an objective point of view.

After you have finished, examine your own feelings once again. Hopefully, your sense of blame will be in better perspective. If you can, forgive those you are blaming. Equally important, forgive yourself. This is the process of reconciliation.

Put away your materials for a while, perhaps a few weeks, perhaps longer. You may return to this process as a natural part of your journal reviews on a monthly, quarterly or annual basis. You may also simply feel that it is time to come back and review the activities again at some other time. This can be a particulary useful exercise when a similar event occurs in your life. Perhaps the same type of argument with a colleague, perhaps the same type of personal failure. In any case, continue as needed until you can feel some peace with yourself and that you are no longer 'haunted' or 'possessed' by the experience.

By going through this process you should be able to gain some clarity and hopefully some peace of mind. You should also have a better understanding of how the events of the past are part of your present. It is especially important to remember as you assess the events of the past that ultimately everything is based on a desire for happiness. The lesson to be learned from our past is not where to assess blame but rather how to recognise foolishness and how to keep from repeating the same foolishness over and over again.

Resolving the imbalances associated with past events is not an easy thing, however, nor a quickly remedied thing. Many emotional patterns have been developed over decades. You will not get over them in a day or so. It is important therefore that you have patience. If you find, for instance, that even after several sessions you still can't completely resolve an emotional conflict, put the exercise aside for a while – a few weeks, a few months, perhaps as long as a year. At some time in the future you will once again be reminded of your painful memories. At this time, return to the exercise and see if you can work with it more successfully.

The Sequential Exercises

After you have been doing the daily exercises for a while and are feeling comfortable with them, you can begin doing this series of sequential exercises. The entire series, if done exactly as planned here, takes about two years. In actuality, it will probably take you longer, but try to complete them within at least three years.

For each exercise there is one or more accompanying chapters in Part 1. You might find it useful to re-read these chapters before you begin each exercise.

The Schedule

Exercise	Weeks	Timing
Breathing	1	10 minutes, twice a day
Feeling	2–3	30–45 minutes, once a day
Golden Gate of Compassion	4–5	30 minutes, once a day
The Outer Elements		
Earth	6–8	30–40 minutes, once a day, six days a week
Water	9–11	30–40 minutes, once a day, six days a week
Fire	12–14	30–40 minutes, once a day, six days a week
Air	15–17	30–40 minutes, once a day, six days a week

Exercise	Weeks	Timing
Space	18–20	30–40 minutes, once a day, six days a week
Integration	21–22	30–40 minutes, once a day, six days a week

The Healing Lights

Exercise	Weeks	Timing
Healing the Body: The White Light	23–25	30–45 minutes, once a day, six days a week
Healing Speech: The Red Light	26–28	30–45 minutes, once a day, six days a week
Healing the Mind: The Blue Light	29–31	30–45 minutes, once a day, six days a week
Holiday	32–33	
'Positive/Negative' Contemplation	34–37 (alternate days with 'The Mirror')	15–20 minutes, once a day, three to four days a week
The Mirror	34–37 (alternate days with '+/- Contemplation')	45 minutes, once a day, three to four days a week
The Golden Potential Within	38–40	50–60 minutes, once a day, six times a week; plus 60 minutes' quality time immediately after each session
The Friend	41–43	about 45–55 minutes, once a day, six times a week
The Enemy	44–47	about 45–55 minutes, once a day, six times a week
Expanding/Contracting	48–51	about 45 minutes, once a day, six times a week
Rainbow	52–54	about 45 minutes, once a day, six times a week
Holiday	55	
Review of the Outer Elements	56–60	about 45 minutes, once a day, six times a week

The Inner Elements

Exercise	Weeks	Timing
Earth	61–64	about 45 minutes, once a day, six times a week

Exercise	Weeks	Timing
Air	65–68	about 45 minutes, once a day, six times a week
Water	69–72	about 45 minutes, once a day, six times a week
Fire	73–76	about 45 minutes, once a day, six times a week
Space	77–80	about 45 minutes, once a day, six times a week
Integration	81–84	about 45 minutes, once a day, six times a week
Universal Compassion	85–88	about 45 minutes, once a day, six times a week

Breathing

Schedule: Week 1.

Timing: 10 minutes, twice a day.

Posture: Sitting on the floor or in a chair with your back straight, or standing with your feet slightly apart. If you can, find a window with an open view or a bare wall to look at.

Everyone knows how to breathe. Or at least they think they do. But just like the way everyone walks and talks differently, the way a person breathes can tell a great deal about his or her current feelings – and about their habitual state of mind.

Everyone can remember a time when they were so frightened that it took their breath away. On the other hand, everyone has had the experience of standing outside in a peaceful country spot early in the morning and taking a deep breath of clean, fresh air. There are lots of ways to breathe. There are ways to breathe which can excite you; there are also ways to breathe which can relax you.

Before moving on to the rest of the exercises in this book it is important to learn a basic breathing exercise to help you achieve a greater sense of relaxation and comfort. This exercise need take only five or ten minutes, and should be done before beginning any of the other exercises in this book. But it is also good to do at any time when you feel the need to relax.

The exercise involves a series of slow and deep in-breaths and out-breaths. If you are feeling particularly agitated or distracted, begin by taking a moment to focus yourself as best you can. Relax your shoulders. Put your hands palm down on your knees, or loosely in your pockets if you are standing in an airport lounge, say, or at a railway station. Try to sense your body settling, as if your weight is shifting lower into your body.

Begin by inhaling slowly and evenly through your nose. Breathe in a little more deeply than usual and hold the breath in for a moment or two. Then exhale, preferably through your mouth, again slightly more deeply and slowly than usual. Each time you breathe out imagine that all the junk inside you, all the stuff that is dragging you down, leaves you and dissolves in the air as grey smoke. Conversely, when you breathe in, breathe in the fresh air that you remember from the country morning. Imagine it refreshing your body and mind.

Repeat the cycle at least five times. If you have more time, repeat it up to twenty-one times, or until you're feeling relaxed.

After you complete the exercise, don't jump up immediately (unless they're calling your flight or your train has arrived). Instead, remain calm for a minute or two. Try to notice the difference in your perception. See if you can be more aware of your surroundings and your body. Throughout the day, as tensions arise, try to recall this feeling. If you can, repeat the exercise from time to time throughout the day.

For the first week of the Sequential Exercises you will probably find it enough to do this exercise – in its longer form – twice a day. This will help you to get into the habit of doing the exercises as well as provide you with a gentle introduction to setting a schedule for relaxation.

Feeling

Schedule: Weeks 2–3.

Timing: 30–45 minutes, once a day.

Posture: Lie on the floor or another reasonably firm surface. A bare floor will probably be too uncomfortable. A yoga mat or a folded blanket is good. If you are older or if you have back problems, you might need a supporting pillow under your knees or at the small of your back. In any case, make sure that you are in a comfortable position which you can maintain for the entire duration of the exercise. Your body should be symmetrical, hands at your side with your palms up. Shoulders level. Try to maintain as much contact with the floor as possible.

This exercise requires that you be relatively alert, not too tired. It is definitely not an exercise that you should attempt late at night after a difficult day. The only exception might be if you want to do it in bed as a means to fall asleep, which is fine, but only as long as you also do it at a more alert time.

In getting to know yourself, one of the first things you need to rediscover is your body and how your thoughts are intertwined with its physical manifestations. Work, especially office work, tends to lead to living 'from the neck up'. Far more attention is paid to mental constructs than to the interaction between your body and the world. Signals that your body sends out – both the good ones and the bad ones – are ignored. This exercise can be useful in helping overcome this.

Begin by spending a moment relating with your surroundings. Sense the floor underneath you. Feel the contact points with your body. Take a deep breath or two. Try to feel a sense of grounding.

First, draw your attention down to the lower part of your body, all the way to your big toes. Be there. Try to sense your toes. You may be able to do this but if not, don't worry. Spend a moment with your big toes, then proceed to the rest of your toes, paying attention to both feet at the same time. Then proceed to your feet, and then your ankles, each time keeping your attention with that particular portion of your body. This process should be rather slow. Spend several minutes with each place in your body that you visit. Give yourself a chance to really experience it.

As you move upward through your body, each time you pause – at calves, knees, thighs, hips, and so on – pay attention to your physical feelings. Is there pain or well-being? Is there tension? An ache? Perhaps a memory of any of these? If you are older or perhaps more accident-prone, is there a memory of past injuries, a scar, a feeling associated with that portion of your body? Pay attention to emotional feelings too. We are all familiar with how we carry tension and worry in our shoulders and necks. But is there other emotional baggage that is carried around too? Perhaps fear stored in the pit of your stomach, or anger in your throat.

As you proceed with this exercise, pause and acknowledge your physical and emotional feelings. Don't, however, spend time analysing them. This is not the time for 'why', nor for 'who did what when', just the time for discovering that you do have feelings and that your body is intricately part of this experience.

Work through your body systematically. When you reach your head and neck, for instance, pay attention to both the outside and the inside: your nose, inside your nostrils; your mouth, inside your mouth. This entire process should take 30 to 40 minutes.

When you get to the top of your head, pause, and then reverse the exercise, working from the top of your head down to your feet and toes. This time, however, proceed at a much quicker pace – it should take less than a minute. Imagine that your body is filled with liquid which is draining out through your toes. Follow the 'water level' as it moves downwards through your body, paying attention to all of the portions of your body that it passes. Imagine that all your aches and pains wash away as the water drains out through your toes.

Now become aware of your breath as you breathe normally. Sense how the in-breath 'touches' each portion of your body. Sense the reaction of your body with the out-breath. Continue watching your breath for another five minutes or so. Then slowly begin stretching. Wiggle your toes and fingers. Flex your calves, shrug your shoulders. Think about how a cat stretches itself when it wakes up.

When you are ready, sit up and then begin your normal activities, trying to take some portion of self-awareness along with you. Pay attention to how your body is moving, perhaps, or the pressure of your feet on the floor. Try to keep this awareness with you for another ten minutes or so.

Golden Gate of Compassion

Schedule: Weeks 4–5.

Timing: 30 minutes, once a day.

Posture: Sitting on the floor with a cushion or on a chair. It is best done with your eyes open or staring out into space at the horizon.

With this exercise, the potential within for transformation and self-healing becomes clear. Everything that is needed for personal happiness and self-fulfilment is already within you. Nothing else is needed.

Many people see transformation as a process of throwing away everything and replacing it with something new or different, the way they might change their clothes each season. It is as if it is necessary to be transported to another plane to be happy. But the truth is that it is those very qualities that manifest as so much craziness and confusion that act as the key to transformation. It is as if within all the junk there is a precious jewel. With this exercise, you realise that this jewel is already present, always there to help when called on. Unless you have this faith in your own self-healing capabilities you really can't take responsibility for your own happiness and self-fulfilment.

Begin by doing the 'Breathing' exercise on pages 117–8, then imagine yourself seated on a hill or the shore of a lake or ocean, somewhere where you can see for vast distances. Imagine that the sky is a clear, cloudless deep blue. Alternatively, imagine a clear, moonless night with a sky full of stars. Spend a few minutes getting comfortable with this image. It shouldn't be solid. You are not trying to create a hallucination, just a sense of being there. Sense the relaxation and peace which you have experienced in the past when you were in such an environment.

After a moment imagine a light in the sky, far off in the distance, a golden light which approaches you. Once it is at a comfortable distance you can see that it is a golden gate, open and inviting.

At this point, become aware of your breathing, paying attention to the movement of your breath through your body. Pay attention, too, to whatever you are feeling. If you have written your journal already today, recall your emotional state. As you breathe out imagine all the good things, bad things, and just plain confusing things leaving your body. Imagine it all leaving your body as a dark cloud of smoke and travelling into space towards the golden gate and finally through it. As it goes through the gate, the smoke becomes transformed into a golden light, almost like golden rain.

This golden, luminous rain falls back on you lightly and gently. It is the embodiment of loving kindness and compassion. It contains all the healing qualities that you need, all the things you need to feel wanted and appreciated. It is important to feel that absolutely anything that comes up in your mind – any feeling, any memory – can be transformed in this way. As feelings and memories emerge, send everything, without exception, through the gate and let it be transformed into golden light.

During this exercise, it is not necessary to focus on the in-breath. If you do, however, then feel as if you are breathing in fresh, clean, purifying air. Everything around you is transformed into freshness and purity by the golden light and rain.

As this golden, luminous rain falls on you, imagine that it transforms your body, speech and mind. Everything about you becomes golden. Everything is all right, just the way it is. Imagine as the rain falls on you that you become filled with its golden light, and become transformed. As this happens, the dark smoke representing your thoughts and feelings becomes lighter and lighter.

When you can feel your own self-healing and transformation taking effect, then think too of all the people you know who could also benefit from some compassion and loving kindness in their life. Imagine that you are feeling so much comfort and self-satisfaction that there is room to accommodate everyone else. Imagine the golden rain spreading out into space to fall on to them as well. Sense that there is no one who is outside your capacity to help. The golden rain reaches everyone in need.

Once you have a sense of everyone, everywhere, being helped and satisfied; that the world, the universe is completely covered with this golden luminous light, then let the golden gate recede back into space. Let it reduce to a tiny speck in the distance and then finally disappear altogether.

At this time the exercise is technically finished. Sit for a while, however, enjoying the sensation. You should feel some sort of relaxation and satisfaction. Savour it for a moment and then stretch and go about your regular activities. If you can, take some of the sense of well-being with you into the rest of the day or evening – you will probably need it.

The Outer Elements

For most people, direct experience of the elements consists mainly of dashing from their car to their air-conditioned/ heated office, battling with them on the roads or shovelling them out of driveways. Life is just a little bit too civilised. The following exercises are a way to get in touch with Earth – and yourself along the way. These exercises can be done on your back patio. But they can also be done as 'field trips'. Indeed, you should do at least one or two sessions of each element in nature. Feel free to use your imagination when deciding how you will experience each of the elements.

For the months that you are doing these exercises, in between the 'formal' sessions, try to pay attention to the elemental qualities in your environment. You might find it interesting, for instance, to explore the use of element words in your vocabulary. What does it mean, after all, to say that someone is 'earthy' or has a 'fiery' personality?

In addition to doing these exercises as part of the normal sequence, you may find them particularly enjoyable on a retreat. They can be especially therapeutic in a natural setting such as a forest or at the beach.

The Outer Elements: Earth

Schedule: Weeks 6–8.

Timing: 30–40 minutes, once a day, six days a week.

To begin this exercise, start small in about a square foot of good old basic soil, the garden variety, preferably a little moist. Place the soil, heaped into a mound, on a large sheet of paper or a piece of plastic. Now just sit there and look at it. Contemplate the 'soilness' of it, the fundamental qualities of earth. Think about stability, heaviness, solidity. Think about these qualities in yourself.

At some time in the week try to make an excursion to a big pile of earth. This may be a mountain, or a sand pile at the local cement factory. Contemplate the earth qualities of the pile.

During the second week, begin the exercise again with the pile of soil mounded up at the centre of the paper or plastic. Again, experience the feelings of 'soilness'. But now use your hands to very slowly level out the soil, spreading it evenly over the sheet of paper. Spread it out until the mound is completely gone. Pay attention to how you feel. Does the soil have the same qualities when it is spread out on the paper as it did when it was mounded up? How do you feel about it?

If you can, take a trip to a place where the earth has been eroded, perhaps a little hillside that has been washed away, perhaps an empty car park. Again, pay attention to your feelings. Try in particular to identify the differences between how you felt about earth in the previous week and how you feel now.

For the final week again use the mound of soil. This time, do the exercise of mounding the soil and then spreading it out very quickly, perhaps in ten minutes. Then rebuild the mound, making sure that all the soil is included back in the 'mountain' once again. Repeat this sequence two or three times. Pay attention to how you feel. Try to notice if there is any difference in your feelings between the mountain stage and the levelling stage.

If you have a chance, go somewhere where the earth is being moved, perhaps at a construction site. Spend some time observing the movement of earth from one location to another. Pay attention to how you feel about it. Think about how you feel in comparison with when you saw a mountain or when you saw eroded earth.

The Outer Elements: Water

Schedule: Weeks 9–11.

Timing: 30–40 minutes, once a day, six days a week.

It's valuable to work with both still and moving water. Begin first by finding a source of moving water. Fountains in parks are particularly wonderful, so too are streams and rivers. At home, just watching the water pour into the bath will work well.

Spend a week with sources of gently moving water. Begin your exploration by considering the qualities of the water: its fluidity, cohesiveness, adaptability. Consider how its characteristics differ from those of earth. Recognise the flexibility. Move your hands through it, listen to it. Try working with water in terms of your own emotions. Look at the potential of water to wash away problems. Let your mind go with the water. Notice how you feel. For your field trip, visit a fountain or a small brook.

For the second week do the exercise with still water – ponds, swimming pools, a dish of water. Again, look at your feelings and explore the qualities of water in this state. How does water in a still state differ from water when it is moving? For your field trip, go to a large lake and just sit by it for a while.

For the final week, work with rapidly moving water, water moving in torrents. Again, repeat the reflective exercises. Notice how you feel. Examine the qualities of water, especially when it is moving violently. Pay particular attention to your energy levels when you are around these type of water sources. If you can, try to visit a location where water is moving rapidly and powerfully – ocean waves crashing on to a cliff; a waterfall; or perhaps you could stand outside in a violent rainstorm.

The Outer Elements: Fire

Schedule: Weeks 12–14.

Timing: 30–40 minutes, once a day, six days a week.

When you work with fire, examine the fire qualities – light, heat, energy, consumption of fuel. Notice also its insubstantiality. Examine, for instance, the differences between earth, water, and fire. Notice the lack of solidity of fire.

For this exercise begin with small, 'tame' sources of fire, then progress to more dramatic representations. For the first week use a candle, a piece of incense, a match held to a cigar – a small source that you can look at directly for a short period of time. Don't, however, spend too much time looking directly into an open flame.

For the second week, try to find a medium-size fire. If it is cool outside, a fire in the hearth is perfect. Just pull up your chair and contemplate the nature of the flames, the heat, the light. Try to determine what the fire quality is in terms of your own personality. If it is summer, you might start a small campfire. If it is very hot, you might also contemplate the heat from the sun on your back, the burning qualities on your skin.

For the final week, try to find an even larger source of fire. If you like you can consider newspaper cuttings about fires that are out of control. Build a big bonfire. Think about the qualities of the sun, a fire so big it's hard to conceive of.

As you do these fire exercises, notice the different qualities of a fire in a small, medium and large fire. Notice the differences in quality between 'warm' and 'hot'. It's not a good idea to live too dangerously nor is arson to be encouraged, but if the opportunity comes up, looking at buildings on fire, forest fires and volcanoes can be a powerful experience. You might also want to visit a place where a fire has occurred recently – say, a burned-out forest or building.

The Outer Elements: Air

Schedule: Weeks 15–17.

Timing: 30–40 minutes, once a day, six days a week.

The primary quality of air is movement. Air can't be seen, only its effects felt. With air, another level of insubstantiality is explored.

Again, this exercise starts with looking at small effects of air, then moving to larger, more dramatic ones. Begin by finding a place where you can experience a gentle breeze. If it is a quiet summer day, this may be sitting outside in a lounge chair. If it is cooler or the breeze is brisker, you might choose to sit inside next to an open window.

Consider the characteristics of air: movement, change, insubstantiality. Observe the movements of animals and objects in relation to air. Notice the flight of birds; notice leaves and scraps of paper. Notice, too, your feelings. Notice the relaxation that you feel when you experience a cool breeze or how invigorating a fresh blast of cold air can be.

In the next two weeks, as with fire, contemplate the degrees of air. See how the qualities change as they increase in degree. Notice the difference between a gentle breeze and a wind storm or tornado. Notice, too, the difference between stale air and fresh air. For a few days find a place where the air is stuffy and stale, not moving. Spend time observing your feelings in this situation. Pay particular attention to your energy levels. Then spend a few days experiencing just the opposite – a place where the air is fresh and invigorating.

At some time while you are doing this exercise, visit a place where the air is especially invigorating, somewhere where you can feel a fresh breeze on your face. A walk by the sea or to the top of a hill can be particularly effective. Observe your feelings. Think about the air phrases in our vocabulary. What does it mean to be 'air-headed' or for something to be like 'a fresh breeze'? What about the words 'stale' or 'stuffy'?

The Outer Elements: Space

Schedule: Weeks 18–20.

Timing: 30–40 minutes, once a day, six days a week.

In the West, space is not considered to be one of the elements. In the East, however, it is considered to be the last of them. Its key qualities are its lack of form, taste and smell; its invisibility, its apparent lack of substance. What space does provide for us, however, is the container within which all the other elements operate. Space represents the relationships and positioning between the elements.

Begin this exercise as you have the others, by working with a rather small, commonplace setting. For the first week you might want to visit familiar places – where you do your daily contemplations, for instance, or where you work. Sit quietly and be aware of the 'space' around you. Notice how the lack or presence of it affects you. Does a room feel small on some days but on others feel spacious? What does it mean to feel constricted? Or claustrophobic? What does cosy mean?

Explore the holding quality of the space. How does this vary from one space to another?

In the next two weeks, concentrate on larger, open spaces. Begin by looking out of a window. Imagine that you can see an infinitely great distance – far, far out into space. Contemplate the arrangement of the other elements within this space. Spend at least one of your contemplations outside, looking into the evening or early morning sky. Contemplate the vastness and the relative proportions of everything within this space.

For your field trip, find somewhere with a panoramic view, or an unusual building whose architecture seems to evoke the concept of space. Explore your feelings in these spaces. Do you feel elevated and inspired? Or do you feel insecure and perhaps a bit anxious?

The Outer Elements: Integration

Schedule: Weeks 21–22.

Timing: 30–40 minutes, once a day, six days a week.

To conclude the outer or physical elements exercises, spend a final fortnight contemplating the relationships between the elements and examining how they interact with each other.

For each day of this exercise, choose a different location, indoors or out, and try to find some variety in the locations. In each case, observe the interplay and balancing of the elements. Explore the meanings of 'harmony' and 'disharmony'. See, too, how in certain environments one element may be more dominant than another. Are there ever occasions where one or more of the elements is completely missing?

Also observe how the elements work with each other. Notice that air and fire tend to work together, mixing and strengthening each other. The same is not true of fire and water or earth and air. The two elements air and fire tend to be upward and outward moving while earth and water tend to be downward and inward moving. Think about how these elements are reflected in your own personality and in the personalities of the people around you. As you move from location to location during this contemplation, observe how each location might affect the people who visit it. Would they be likely to feel uplifted, invigorated and inspired, or suppressed, stifled and deadened? Would they feel fuzzy and unfocused or grounded and secure?

Notice the healthy qualities of the elements as well as their unhealthy qualities. What makes one experience of the elements healthy and another unhealthy?

The Healing Lights

As you keep your journal and follow the exercises it is likely that memories will come to the surface. Many of these memories will be pleasant, but many will recall past experiences of pain, embarrassment or discomfort. Some of the memories may have been suppressed because they were simply too intense to deal with. The following three exercises provide a means to cope with and heal pains from the past. They are also a very effective way to cope with emotional imbalances as they arise in the present. Each exercise should be carefully prepared for and concluded in the same way, as described below.

Before beginning this sequence, it may be helpful to return to the 'Feeling' exercise on pages 118–20 for one or two sessions. This may help you to get in touch with your emotions and with your memories of past pains.

Preparation

Posture: Sitting posture with your back straight. If possible, find a place where you can look out of a window. Spend a few moments relaxing with the 'Breathing' exercise on page 117.

With your eyes open and gazing into the distance, imagine that you are seated beneath either a clear, blue, cloudless daytime sky or a clear, moonless night-time sky full of stars. Relax for a moment. If you can, become aware of your mental, physical and emotional states. Spend a moment assessing your dominant emotion or pain. Try to assess where you are holding it in your body. Is it in your throat, your shoulders, the pit of your stomach?

Then imagine that in the distance there is a tiny dot of light. This dot of light moves through space towards you. As it approaches, it becomes a sphere of light composed of five brilliant, clear, distinct colours – white, yellow, green, blue and red. These colours represent the pure essences and elements of our being. They move together in total harmony and balance, swirling across the surface of the sphere.

Recognise that this sphere of light contains all the healing qualities that are needed for life. It has the capability to cure any imbalance and to heal any wound. If you have strong religious or spiritual beliefs, you can think of this light as the essence of whatever deity you feel attached to. Otherwise, recognise it as the essence of compassion and loving kindness universally present throughout the world.

Once the sphere is at a comfortable distance from you, imagine that the five colours turn into a single colour, depending on the exercise that you are doing. In each case, choose a shade that is clear and bright and inspiring for you. The single colour then radiates from the sphere towards you and enters your body as described in the individual exercises below.

Conclusion

Conclude all three exercises in the same way. After a certain period of time, your body should feel light and transparent. You should feel that all the pain has evaporated as dark smoke. Gradually the smoke leaving your body becomes clear. (Even if you don't actually feel this way, continue as if you did.)

At this point, the light is reabsorbed back into the sphere, which returns to its initial five colours, all swirling on the surface. Think of the sphere now as containing the combined healing qualities of the universe as well as your own healing capabilities.

The sphere then shrinks into the distance until, once again, it is a small dot of light, which disappears into the clear sky.

Conclude the exercise with a few minutes of unfocused thought. Just relax, letting the mind rest until thoughts return. Then resume your normal activities, trying to carry the warm feeling that you have from the exercise into whatever you are doing.

Healing the Body: The White Light

Schedule: Weeks 23–25.

Timing: 30–45 minutes, once a day, six days a week.

The white light heals physical pain, both past and present. This light is particularly effective when you are feeling physically exhausted or burned out. It is also helpful for physical tension brought on by stress or long hours and is useful for jet lag.

The white light enters the body first through the forehead. (If this is uncomfortable for you, you can bring the light into your body with the in-breath.) It then spreads through the rest of the body but especially to those areas where the pain is held. When you do the exercise, try to find where you are holding tension in your body. Send the light to this location. If you are exhausted, become aware of the heaviness and listlessness of your body and of the light washing away that heaviness.

As the light moves through you, allow all the physical pain and tension to leave your body on the out-breath as a dark grey smoke that dissipates into the atmosphere.

Continue doing the exercise until you have a sense of physical lightness and relief. The solidity and heaviness of the body should also be diminished. You should be left feeling physically refreshed.

Towards the end of the session, if you can, think about other people you know who are also experiencing physical pain – perhaps someone in your family, or someone that you work with. Imagine that the white light from the sphere is going out to them as well. Imagine that it is having the same effect on them as it is having on you. Then think about all the physical suffering in the world, all the wars, disasters, famines. Send out the white light to everyone who is experiencing physical pain.

Healing Speech: The Red Light

Schedule: Weeks 26–28.

Timing: 30–45 minutes, once a day, six days a week.

The red light heals feelings of frustration and dissatisfaction. It is associated with speech because it deals with blocks to expression. It is particularly useful when you feel unfulfilled, or that your value to others is not appreciated. It is also effective after you have lost a project to the competition or after a promotion has gone to someone else. It is a particularly good remedy for feelings of bitterness and resentment.

The red light enters the body first through the base of the throat (or, alternatively, on the in-breath). It then spreads through the rest of the body but especially to those areas where the frustration is held. When you do the exercise, try to find where you are holding the feelings in your body. If you are feeling resentful, for example, think of the resentment and then analyse where in your body you are feeling tense. Send the light to this location.

As the light moves through the body, all the dissatisfaction and frustration leaves it on the out-breath as a dirty reddish-brown smoke that dissipates into the atmosphere.

Doing this exercise should leave you with a feeling of loving kindness and openness. Continue until you have this sense of being fulfilled and satisfied. This openness should extend to feeling able to express yourself and feeling able to accept the openness of others.

As with the white light exercise, spend the last portion thinking about similar feelings which other people are having. Perhaps people you work with who have shared the same frustrating or disappointing experiences with you. Think then too of all the people throughout the world who are in the same situation or far worse. Perhaps think about people who are denied freedom of expression.

Healing the Mind: The Blue Light

Schedule: Weeks 29–31.

Timing: 30–45 minutes, once a day, six days a week.

The blue light heals feelings of extreme mental pain. It heals fear, embarrassment and mental confusion. It is also appropriate for feelings of anger and rage that are the result of fear or of being threatened. It is particularly useful when you have a difficult decision to make or when your future seems very uncertain, perhaps if you have lost your job or if you are afraid of being reassigned. It is also extremely effective during times of extreme or unpredictable change and is the remedy for anxiety attacks.

The blue light enters the body first at the heart-centre (or on the in-breath). It then spreads through the rest of the body but especially to those areas where the fear or anger is held. When you do the exercise, try to find where you are holding these feelings. Send the light to this location.

As the light moves through the body, all these feelings leave as a thick, blue-black smoke that dissipates into the atmosphere.

Doing this exercise should leave you with a feeling of courage and confidence. Your anxiety should be gone or reduce, and your anger should be diminished. You should feel as if you have the ability to cope with whatever situation may arise.

Conclude this exercise by thinking about people you know who are experiencing the same kinds of fear, anxiety or anger. Then think about all the people in the world who are trapped in these experiences. Send the blue light in their direction.

Note

After completing this first sequence of the exercises, you can use them at any other time when you feel the need. Use them in the same way that you might use a pain-relief tablet or cough syrup. Apart from the normal sitting posture, they can also be done in bed, either falling asleep or on waking.

Holiday

Schedule: Weeks 32–33.

After a while, any schedule, no matter how useful, can start to get a little stale and burdensome. So give yourself a break for a few weeks. Do something different, relax. At the end of your break, note in your journal how you feel about returning to the exercises – and perhaps how you felt immediately before the holiday.

Positive/Negative Contemplation

Schedule: Weeks 34–37 (alternate days with 'The Mirror', pages 136–8).

Timing: 15–20 minutes, once a day, three to four days a week.

Posture: Find somewhere quiet and sit cross-legged on the floor with the paper (see below) in front of you within easy reach. If you like, you can also do this sitting at your desk or dining-room table with the paper on the table in front of you. Remember to sit with your back straight.

The object of this exercise is to gain some awareness of your attitudes, especially those that manifest themselves habitually.

Often people suffer from mood swings or have something 'cooking' inside which they are not even aware of. Not until it streams to the surface do they realise just how bad it is. They can walk around angry for days, weeks or months without even being aware of the mood that is being projected. This exercise will help you to see your thought patterns. If you like, you can do it in place of writing your journal. Just perhaps make a note in your journal about the results of the exercise. Try to select different times during the day so that you can note your moods as well as how busy or still your mind can be.

You will need a large blank sheet of paper. A page from a flip chart is perfect but the back of a grocery bag will work equally well. Get a large marker pen that writes easily with just a touch on the paper. Draw a horizontal line from left to right midway across the page. (You might want to set up a stack of these pages in advance.)

Begin by doing the 'Breathing' exercise on pages 117–8. Then try to just be there, present with yourself, as gently and as peacefully as possible.

Holding the marker pen in your hand, begin to observe your thoughts as they arise. Very gently make a quick judgement on each thought. Was it a positive thought, a negative thought, or just neutral? For positive thoughts, place a mark above the line; for negative, a mark below the line; for neutral thoughts, a mark on the line. For the positive and negative marks the space from the line should be in proportion to the degree of the feeling.

Try to space out the marks according to the speed at which thoughts are coming. You will probably find that there is a lot more space between the marks at the beginning of the session than there is later on – unless of course you fall asleep.

From time to time, you might want to vary the duration of this exercise. You might find it useful to see if your mind starts to slow down after you have been sitting for a while. Or you may detect a pattern of ups and downs.

Date each sheet of paper and keep them together. From time to time, when convenient, take a look at the patterns. Once you have two or more weeks of exercises you might start to see some interesting patterns arising. Are you always angry, and maybe not realising it? Is there a certain time of day when your mind is much calmer, and perhaps happier than at others?

The Mirror

Schedule: Weeks 34–37 (alternate days with 'Positive/Negative Contemplation').

Timing: 45 minutes, once a day, three to four times a week.

Note: This exercise is done during the same time that you are doing the 'Positive/Negative Contemplation' exercise. It may be too intense to do every day, so you should alternate it with the 'Positive/Negative Contemplation'. The objective is to learn some more about how you project your professional persona into the environment.

Everyone is very attached to their persona, so attached that they tend to forget that it is just that, a projection, a fantasy which every other person around conspires to maintain: 'You believe my projection and I'll believe yours.'

A word of caution: some people find this exercise a little disorientating. If this is the case, reduce the number of times you do it during the week. But try to stick with it. This exercise is the precursor of several of the exercises that follow. If it gets to be too much, discontinue it until a later time in the sequential exercises – preferably before you do 'The Friend' and 'The Enemy' exercises on pages 141–6. Continue doing the 'Positive/Negative Contemplation' exercise for the rest of the scheduled time.

As for 'The Healing Lights', some time needs to be spent on preparation, described below, and then the exercise is developed. For the first two weeks do the phase one exercise; for the next two weeks, the phase two exercise.

Preparation

Posture: To do this exercise you will need a mirror large enough to reflect your whole body. Find somewhere to do the exercise where you can sit either cross-legged or in a chair in front of the mirror. Place the mirror so that most or all of your body is visible.

Begin with 'Doing Nothing' (see pages 105–6). When you are finished, observe yourself in the mirror for just a moment. At this time you should 'see' your image as just that, a reflection in the mirror. Just observe, without analysing or judging.

Now either close your eyes or look down. Concentrate on being aware of your thoughts in much the same way that you have been doing during 'Positive/Negative Contemplation'. Watch without analysing the play of ideas, thoughts and emotions as they run through your mind. Continue with this for about ten minutes.

Phase One (the first two weeks)

Look back up into the mirror, continuing to be aware of your thoughts. As your thoughts and emotions arise, send them into your image in the mirror. Send everything that is 'you', both positive and negative, into the mirror image.

As you do this, try to develop a sense of separation and insubstantiality with regard to your thoughts and emotions. Try to let go of your ownership. Try to let go of their solidity. Imagine that it is not just your visual image but your entire persona that is in the mirror. Send your thoughts and emotions with each out-breath. Send everything. Continue doing this for about ten minutes.

Now observe the persona in the mirror. This includes all your good and bad qualities, the person you hide from the world, the person you project as your business persona, everything. Then with your in-breath return to yourself, the 'true you', from the image in the mirror. Return to yourself the qualities that are positive and are genuine. Leave behind the projections and the fantasy persona. Leave behind the negative qualities that diminish you. As you do this, be aware that you are choosing the qualities that you wish to retain and those that you wish to abandon. Continue with this portion of the exercise for about ten to fifteen minutes.

Phase Two (the second two weeks)

Look back up into your image in the mirror. This time as you breathe out, breathe yourself, your thoughts and emotions into the mirror image. On the in-breath, breathe in the thoughts and emotions from the mirror image. With each in- and out-breath exchange yourself with the mirror image.

As you work with this phase of the exercise, keep in mind that you are working with your projections. You are working with the thoughts and emotions that you continually project into the world. You are also working with projections of other people's thoughts and emotions as they are directed towards you. As you observe the to and fro of these projections, try to develop a sense of insubstantiality about them. It is not important at this time to analyse the contents of these projections: simply be aware of your thoughts and emotions as projections. Again, continue with this portion of the exercise for about ten to fifteen minutes.

Conclusion

At the conclusion of the exercise, either close your eyes or look down. Relax. Let your thoughts flow. If you like, after a few minutes you can get up and walk to a window. Stand or sit quietly and gaze out towards the horizon. Try to be aware of the flow of your thoughts as they arise and then fall away.

The Golden Potential Within

Schedule: Weeks 38–40.

Timing: 50–60 minutes, once a day, six times a week; plus 60 minutes' quality time immediately after each session.

Posture: The first part of the session involves sitting somewhere quiet where you can be assured of not being interrupted. If possible, find somewhere where you can look out of a window. Choose a sitting posture, either cross-legged on the floor or sitting on a rigid chair. Make sure that your back is straight but not too tense. Pull your shoulders back. If you like, you can put your hands palm down on your knees or thighs. This can be helpful to remind you to keep your back straight and not to slouch.

It is important that everyone has confidence in their basic goodness so they can act outwards from that core with compassion and understanding. This exercise helps you to get in touch with those qualities.

For this exercise you will need to allow approximately two hours each day. So unless you get up very early in the morning or you are on holiday (when it's a good exercise to do), you will want to do this exercise in the evening.

The exercise is done in two parts, one immediately following the other. The first part involves a formal session that needs to be done alone in silence. The second part is informal, something akin to what might be called quality time.

For the three weeks of this exercise it is highly recommended that you turn off the television set, all the computer games and anything else in the category of 'mindless entertainment'. Cut the cord if you have to. Set the video recorder for all the good programmes.

Begin by doing one of the 'Breathing' exercises (see pages 117–8). If you are feeling emotionally charged, then do it a bit longer until you start to feel settled. For the next five minutes or so, contemplate the qualities of goodness that you value. Honesty, bravery, sensitivity, compassion, selflessness, gentleness . . . . Think of these qualities and how having them enriches your life and the life of others.

Half close your eyes. Try to imagine that your body is light and transparent, not solid. If you like, you can do another cycle of the breathing exercise, but this time on the out-breath breathe out your solidity and heaviness.

Now imagine that there is a light, shimmering yellow lotus flower suspended inside you at your heart-centre. This flower is open, its petals unfolded. It is extremely beautiful, almost dreamlike. Now imagine that above this flower is a transparent, colourless, hollow tube. This tube runs through the centre of your body from just above the centre of the lotus all the way to the top of your head. At the crown of your head it opens out into a funnel shape. Keep the image very light and transparent, like the reflection of clouds in a lake.

Hold this image for a minute or two. Now imagine that a transparent, golden, sphere of light appears, poised just above the top of your head, above the mouth of the funnel. This sphere of light contains all the qualities of goodness that you value. If you have strong religious beliefs, then you can exchange this sphere of light for a deity or religious figure that you cherish. Instil this sphere or figure with all the qualities that you value.

Now imagine that the sphere of light descends into the mouth of the funnel and down the tube until it reaches the lotus. It then rests at the centre of the yellow lotus. Now you are imbued with all of these qualities. Feel that they are part of you. Hold this image for 30–40 minutes.

As you do this exercise, try to imagine that your body is as light and transparent as possible. None of this should be solid or permanent. If you find that after a while your mind wanders completely away from the exercise, then you can restart it from the point where you first imagined the yellow lotus at your heart-centre.

After you are finished with this portion of the exercise, spend a few minutes stretching and relaxing where you are sitting. Keep the image of the golden sphere at your heart-centre.

Now you can get up and do something. Choose something to do which is contemplative, perhaps gardening, or walking in the woods; taking a bubble bath or manicure; watching the sun set. You can do this alone or with others, provided that the activity isn't too frenetic. If you have small children then give them a bath and read them a story; take older children for a walk with you.

As you do these activities, keep the golden sphere of goodness in your heart. Let it permeate your actions and your thoughts. This is your quality time. Gradually, the farther you get away from the exercise, your thoughts and actions will return to 'normal'. Let this happen at its own pace.

The Friend

Schedule: Weeks 41–43.

Timing: About 45–55 minutes, once a day, six times a week.

Posture: Sitting with a straight back.

Note: Before you start this exercise it is important that you first complete 'The Mirror' on pages 136–8. If you like, you can return to 'The Mirror' and do it for a day or two.

Everyone has favourite people and not-so-favourite people. And we treat favourite people much better than those who aren't so favoured. In general, we do nicer things for them and tolerate their flaws. This can be good and it can be bad. In this exercise, attachments are examined, along with their positive and negative qualities.

Begin the session with 'Breathing', pages 117–8. Spend some time during and after the breathing exercise becoming grounded and relaxed in your surroundings, observing them without making judgements.

Now think of the person who means the most to you in the world. This will probably be someone in your family or someone who you are very emotionally attached to. Perhaps a boyfriend or girlfriend. Spend some time developing a sense of warmth towards this person. Evoke their memory. As you do this you will probably notice some sort of mental image of this person in your mind. Perhaps a glimmer of their face or a gesture that endears them to you. You will also probably begin to feel some emotional intensity. A sense of loving or gratitude.

Expand on this feeling and these images until you have a sense of the person actually being in the room with you, seated in front of you. The person does not have to be aware of you or be paying attention to you. Just evoke their presence in the room. Some people have a very strong visual sense and can actually 'see' the person. For other people this is more difficult. Whether you can actually 'see' the person or not is not incredibly important. What is important is that you have a sense of the presence of the person in the room with you. Their essence.

Spend about ten minutes or so developing this presence. Contemplate the qualities of the person that you admire – perhaps qualities that no one else recognises. Think too of their little flaws and how easy it is to tolerate and forgive them. Develop a sense of openness and trust towards this person.

Now take a break. Relax. Get up if you like and walk around the room. As you do so, try to keep a sense of the person as still being there with you in the room. Then sit down again, face the person and begin the second part of the exercise.

Become aware of your breathing. You should be breathing in a relaxed, normal fashion. As you breathe out, imagine that the essence of yourself is moving into your friend. As you breathe in, imagine that the essence of your friend is moving into you. Exchange yourself with your friend on the in- and out-breaths. It is not necessary to do this on each and every breath. (If you do so, you are likely to start to hyperventilate.)

As you do this exchange, maintain a sense of openness and trust with your friend. There is nothing that you need to hide from each other. There are no secrets between you. You accept each other completely. Warts and all.

Continue exchanging your qualities for 20 to 30 minutes. Be sure to exchange both the positive and the negative qualities. Accept both equally. Maintain the sense of openness and trust. Get to know each other completely.

At the end of the session, relax again. If you like, you can return to being yourself, or you can maintain the presence of your friend. If your friend is someone who is a hero to you, someone you admire deeply and look up to, then keep these admired qualities with you. Resume your normal activities.

Continue the exercise with the same person for the first week. For the second week choose a different person. This time the person should be a close friend but not someone as close to you as your first choice – perhaps a long-time friend or colleague. For the third week choose someone you like but who is not as close to you. If you can, choose someone who you work with.

Each time you do the exercise, repeat the process of evoking the person and then developing a sense of trust and openness with them. As you do the exchange, pay attention to your friend's motivations and world-view. Understand why they do the things that they do. Understand where their strengths and weaknesses come from. Exchange this same information about yourself with them.

The Enemy

Schedule: Weeks 44–47.

Timing: About 45–55 minutes, once a day, six times a week.

Posture: Sitting with a straight back.

At first it may seem that this exercise is totally different from 'The Friend'. In actuality, the two are quite similar. Both deal with attachments to other people and to emotional states. The first is an attachment associated with pleasure; the second an attachment associated with pain. In both cases, the attachment conditions life, sometimes positively, sometimes negatively.

In this exercise, the relationships associated with pain are explored. This can be a very, very scary proposition. You will probably find yourself approaching this exercise with an enormous amount of trepidation and resistance. To cope with this better, during the four weeks that you work on this exercise you may find it beneficial to spend some time doing artwork and other non-verbal expressive activities. Work with large sheets of paper, sloppy paints and glue. Make a mess.

The exercise starts the same way as 'The Friend', beginning with 'Breathing', pages 117–8. Spend some time becoming grounded and relaxed.

A different type of enemy is examined each week (see below). Begin by examining the nature of this enemy. In this exercise you are not exploring events relating to a particular enemy or type of enemy (use the 'Clarifying Blame' exercise on pages 111–4 if you want to work with individual events). Rather, the focal point is your emotional reactions and the emotional reactions of your enemies. The exercise offers a way to understand yourself and your enemies. This is not about right and wrong.

Begin by exploring your emotional reaction to the particular type of enemy being investigated this week. Examine for a few minutes how you feel about this type of enemy. Examine their characteristics. Then select someone from your past or present who is the best representative of this type of enemy. Continue to do the exercise for the complete week with the same person. It should be someone who you have a strong emotional reaction to. Your pulse should jump; your shoulders should tighten.

Imagine that this enemy is seated in front of you, that this person is present in the room with you. Open yourself up to your feelings about this person. Open yourself up, too, to the emotions of your enemy; how they feel about you. Spend 10 to 15 minutes letting yourself open up to these feelings.

At this point, take a short break. Stretch. Get up and walk around the room. Get a glass of water. Come back to the exercise in about five minutes.

Now begin the second phase of the exercise. Sit facing your enemy and begin the process of exchanging yourselves. Breathe yourself out into your enemy with the out-breath; breathe the enemy into you with your in-breath. Continue this for 20 to 30 minutes. Do this phase of the exercise without too much thinking, analysis or judging. Just exchange the emotional context.

After you have completed this phase of the exercise, spend some time analysing the nature of your relationship. Contemplate the feelings from both points of view. If you feel fearful towards this person, examine the nature of the fear. Where does it come from? What is its source? Look at the fear from your enemy's point of view. Exchange the fear with your enemy.

Do the same if you feel anger or pain. Look at the nature of the pain, at the betrayal. If someone is your enemy through no fault of their own, then examine their feelings. Try to understand the nature of their animosity.

Finally, if you can, examine the positive qualities that can come out of this 'war'. Think of how it can be transformed into something positive. Has this argument taught you a valuable lesson? Has it made you stronger or more humble? Has it helped someone else? If at all possible, develop a sense of gratitude towards your enemy for having given you this opportunity to learn more about yourself and to grow as a person. If you can't do this, then at least develop some understanding and appreciation of the motivations that have driven this person to be who they are. Continue the session until you can develop one of these attitudes.

The Feared Enemy (week 1)

This may or may not be a personal enemy. But it is someone you fear terribly. This is someone who, if you saw him or her coming towards you, you would run from . . . and run fast. If possible, this person should be someone you have a personal relationship with. It may be someone from the present, but it may also be someone from the past whom you have always feared. Perhaps an authority figure of some kind. When you do the exercise, spend time examining the nature of the fear. Try to face it.

The Enemy Who Has Hurt You (week 2)

This is someone who has caused you a great deal of personal pain, either emotional or physical. It may be someone you hate; it may also be someone you love. It is someone you have a tendency to obsess over, someone you can't stop thinking about. When you do the exercise, spend time examining the nature of the obsession. Practise letting go of it.

The Mistaken Enemy (week 3)

This is someone who has become your enemy through no fault of your own. Perhaps someone told a story about you that has resulted in someone having a wrong impression of you. Perhaps someone hates you because of the colour of your skin or the country where you were born or the religion that you practise. When you do the exercise, spend time examining the relationship from the other person's point of view. Try to understand the relationship.

The Cultural or Institutional Enemy (week 4)

This is the enemy that you were brought up to hate. This is a class hatred. Whether because of race, religion or family name, this is a group of people who are your enemies. For this exercise choose someone you know who is a representative of this class of people. As you do the exchange, try to be a member of that class and to see yourself from the opposite perspective.

Expanding/Contracting

Schedule: Weeks 48–51.

Timing: About 45 minutes, once a day, six times a week.

Posture: Sitting comfortably with a straight back.

Change is threatening when it impinges on boundaries. The more rigid and solid those boundaries are, the more likely it is that pain and discomfort are experienced when change occurs.

This exercise and the next one can be helpful in exploring personal boundaries. In doing these exercises, you may recognise the narrowness and rigidity of your personal boundaries and perhaps begin to break through this rigidity, becoming more flexible and tolerant in times of change.

Begin by doing the 'Breathing' exercise on pages 117–8. Then spend some time becoming aware of your surroundings, taking a little more time with this than usual. Notice the pressure of your body against the floor or the chair seat and assess your surroundings and your relationship to them.

Now become gently aware of your breathing without altering your breathing pattern. Just watch yourself breathe normally for a few minutes. At your heart-centre imagine that a tiny, tiny, colourless dot of light appears. As you breathe, notice that on the out-breath this dot of light slowly expands. The expansion should occur on every fourth or fifth breath. As the light becomes larger it becomes a glimmering golden sphere, insubstantial, translucent. This sphere of light continues to grow until it is a comfortable size, about the size of a grapefruit, resting at your heart-centre.

This golden sphere is the essence of goodness and compassion. Pause for a while and just become aware of it resting at your heart-centre. Feel comfortable with it. Imagine that the rest of your body takes on the same translucent, insubstantial qualities as this sphere of light.

Expanding

Now become aware of your normal breathing again. On every fourth or fifth out-breath, imagine that your body and the golden sphere begin to expand. Imagine at first that your body is the size of the room, then the house or building, then a city block, and then a mountain. Spend a moment between each expansion being aware of the sensation. Don't worry about bumping into things. Your body is insubstantial. If this requires a little too much suspension of disbelief, contemplate for a moment the nature of the physical make-up of the universe. Remember school physics and the construction of atoms. At an atomic level, there is a lot more space than matter.

Until your body is the size of a mountain, try to imagine it as pretty much the same shape as your original body. As it becomes larger, however – as large as a city, a country, the planet, the solar system, the galaxy, the universe - imagine it as an amorphous shape. Continue expanding your body for about 20 minutes.

Contracting

Now begin to contract your body. This time on every fourth or fifth in-breath reduce your body in size using approximately the same increments as you used during the expanding phase. During the contracting phase it is not important to maintain the shape of your original body. Concentrate instead on contracting your presence in space. Continue until your presence is back to approximately its original size. Remember that the golden sphere remains at your heart-centre and expands and contracts with you.

Continue contracting, first to half your size, then to half again, and so on. Continue contracting until you and the golden sphere are both the size of the tiny dot of light.

After you have completed the contracting phase, relax, letting your mind drift. Once you are aware of thoughts returning, become aware of your original body. Spend a few minutes being aware of the room and your presence in it. Then continue your normal activities.

Rainbow

Schedule: Weeks 52–54.

Timing: About 45 minutes, once a day, six times a week.

Posture: Sitting comfortably on the floor.

This exercise may require some patience and understanding from your family. (By now, they should be somewhat used to your eccentricities anyway.) It explores the transitory nature of possessions: all those things that are kept or wished for. A great deal of time and energy is spent in the quest for possessions. It takes hard work to get them and then, once acquired, a lot of time is spent caring for them or worrying that someone else will take them away. In this exercise, the value of this activity is explored. Three general categories of objects are explored:

1. *Objects That Were Once of Great Value*
These are objects that are owned and which were once of great value but which now have very little value. They are probably worn-out objects or items that have gone out of fashion. It may be something like a dress which was your pride and joy when first bought but which you now regard with embarrassment or bewilderment. It might also be a piece of furniture or a piece of jewellery.

2. Objects Owned and of Great Value

These are objects that you possess and in which you take great pride, especially status items such as cars and technological gadgets which make you feel important.

3. Objects Desired and of Great Value

These are objects on your 'wish list'. They are the possessions which you dream about having. Again, these are mostly status items which you think will make you feel personally important.

For each week of the exercise choose objects that are representative of the category being explored. You can either work with the same object for the entire week or you can change to different objects each day. If the object is something that you already own, if at all possible do the exercise in the presence of the actual object. If the object is a car, for instance, then do the exercise in the garage; if the object is your new wide-screen television, then do the exercise in front of it (with the set turned off!). If the object is something that you desire but don't own, then make a trip to see the object. Go to the store and look at it. Drive to the building site. Then, if possible, get a picture of the object which you can use during the exercise.

For the exercise, find somewhere to sit where you can see the object but where it does not take up your whole field of vision. If the object is small like a laptop computer or mobile phone, place it on the floor or on a table in front of you. If the object is large like a car or television, sit with the object off to the side so that you can see it at the corner of your vision. If the object is something like a house or a piece of land, do the exercise from a site far enough away so that you can see the property against the skyline.

Sit with your back straight. Spend some time relaxing and doing the 'Breathing' exercise on pages 117–8. Then direct your attention to the object. Spend a few minutes noting its qualities that give you pleasure or that once gave you pleasure. Examine what this object means to you.

Now look away from the object. If the object is small, direct your attention to a space above it. If the object is large, turn to the side. Now imagine the object in front of you in space. If you have ever seen a high-tech movie or television programme, then imagine that the object is like a 3-D holographic image. It hangs suspended in space, you can see it but it's not quite there - just like a rainbow. Construct the image in front of you. If you have a hard time remembering what it looks like, then glance at the real object or the picture of the object.

Spend at least five minutes with this construction. Depending on your personal aptitude, you may have a lot of success in doing this or you may not. If you have trouble doing this type of visualisation, don't worry about it. The most important aspect of this exercise is to imagine that the object is present in space in front of you.

Now slowly destroy the rainbow object. If it is mechanical, take it apart, then break it into pieces. If it is a piece of clothing, take the seams apart, then unweave the fabric and shred the thread. As you do this, examine your feelings towards this object. In particular examine the value of the object. Where is its value to you? How does the change in this object change you? What is your relationship to this object?

Continue destroying the object until it is nothing more than a pile of dust. There is nothing left to identify it as the original object. Now imagine that the pile of dust transforms into a rainbow sphere of five colours: red, yellow, green, white and blue. This sphere has no edges or boundaries. It blends into the space around it. This sphere represents the basic essence of all the elements in perfect harmony. Spend a few minutes appreciating the harmonious balance of this sphere.

After a few minutes, reconstruct the rainbow object once again out of the rainbow colours of the sphere. This time, appreciate the harmonious qualities of the object. Appreciate its relationship to the basic qualities of the elements. Then merge the rainbow object into the real object. The real object is now imbued with the qualities of the rainbow object. Spend a few minutes examining your relationship with the object. Where does its value lie? Does it have value at all? Do you need it? Is it an obstacle or an opportunity for you? Is it worth all the effort you put into acquiring it or keeping it?

You can either spend the entire session working through the cycle of the exercise just once or up to three times. If you do it more than once, take a small break and relax between each cycle.

If you like, after the exercise you can spend some time with the object. If it is a computer or telephone, work with it for a while. If it's a dress, try it on. Explore your relationship to the object.

Through the weeks of this exercise, also explore your relationship with other objects. Re-examine what you need and what you don't need. Examine your attachments. You might, for instance, want to do this exercise just before you plan to buy something.

Holiday

Schedule: Week 55.

It's time for another holiday. Go and enjoy yourself!

Review of the Outer Elements

Schedule: Weeks 56–60.

Timing: About 45 minutes, once a day, six times a week.

Spend a week reviewing each of the outer elements (see pages 123–9). As you do the exercises pay attention to how the elements affect your personality as well as your physical state. Also notice the opposite – how your moods affect your interpretation of the elements. Consider in what ways who and what you are affects the harmony of the elements in your environment. Notice the impact of man on the elements.

You might also want to observe the integration of the elements, how each exists in conjunction with the others. Earth always contains moisture; fire always contains air; but water diminishes the power of fire, and so on.

The Inner Elements

As you work through these exercises, you should be developing a sense of when you are healthy and when you are not so healthy. In this case, health means physical, mental and emotional health. It means a lot more than what might be found on a doctor's report.

Health can be considered in terms of harmony. Are the emotions balanced, are they in harmony? By now, having spent more than a year, maybe nearly two, doing these exercises, you should be in better harmony with yourself and your world. You should also be far more sensitive to when you are in harmony and when you are not. With regard to your physical health, you should now be capable of maintaining an awareness of how you are treating yourself. Are you eating correctly? Exercising sensibly? Are you taking care of yourself to make sure you don't catch a cold? In terms of emotional and mental health, are you taking care of your relationships with other people? Are you paying attention to your emotional state and not becoming too stressed?

In addition to your personal harmony, you should also be able to maintain an awareness of the physical, emotional and mental harmony of those around you - and of the entire world around you. By now you should have a good understanding of how your own harmony or lack thereof affects your environment.

The exercises on the inner elements allow these harmonies to be explored at an even more subtle level. In these exercises the interplay between the elements and your emotional and physical states are explored. These exercises can help to restore balance when there is disharmony; when you are in harmony they can help to increase and refine your personal well-being.

Working with the Inner Elements

Posture: Sitting with a straight back.

Spend at least five minutes doing the 'Breathing' exercise on pages 117–8. Relax. Try to feel a lightness to your body. Spend a few minutes noticing any lack of balance or harmony in yourself. Are you restless, tired, angry, anxious? Don't spend any time analysing the causes, just note the feelings.

For each of the elements you will imagine a coloured geometric form located at the centre of your body at the particular location appropriate for that element. Keep in mind that the form is only made of light; it has no substance. Try to imagine yourself in the same way. Without substance. Light emanates from the object and spreads throughout your body. All the harmonious qualities of the element spread through your body. If you are feeling any particular imbalance, the light particularly works for that area. Any particular impurities or distortions evaporate off the body as a dusty smoke.

Some people have difficulties imagining objects. This is not in any way a reflection on your capabilities, just a matter of how you operate. Don't worry about it. If you do have trouble imagining the particular objects in this exercise, you can alternatively imagine that the light is coming from the particular location in your body. Feeling the presence of the healing qualities of the elements is the most important aspect of this exercise.

About halfway through the exercise, contemplate the qualities of the particular element as they relate to your environment. Consider where there is a lack of harmony or where this particular elemental quality is too weak or too strong. Think too of how the people you know and that you know about could benefit by experiencing a harmonious environment.

Imagine that the light from the elemental object now goes to these people and locations as well. Start first with the people and activities that you are closest to - those you directly work with or that you see each day. Then extend the range of the light from the elemental object within you to include people you know slightly or that you don't see too often. Keep on expanding the range of the light from the sphere until it encompasses everyone you can think of. Imagine the elemental quality in balance throughout the world.

At the end of the exercise imagine that the object dissolves into space. It becomes more and more transparent until it gradually disappears. The harmonious qualities of the element remain with you. Relax for a few minutes, appreciating the balance that you feel.

The Inner Elements: Earth

Schedule: Weeks 61–64.

Timing: About 45 minutes, once a day, six times a week.

The earth element is represented by a yellow cube. This cube is positioned at the centre of the body at the level of the navel. Earth in its harmonious state has the qualities of solidity and stability without heaviness or stubbornness.

The Inner Elements: Air

Schedule: Weeks 65–68.

Timing: About 45 minutes, once a day, six times a week.

Air is represented by an emerald green, half-spherical bowl located in the centre of the body about 10 cm (4 in) below the navel. Air in its harmonious state has the qualities of adaptability and spontaneous insight and intelligence.

The Inner Elements: Water

Schedule: Weeks 69–72.

Timing: About 45 minutes, once a day, six times a week.

Water is imagined as a white sphere located in the centre of the body at the level of the heart. Water in its harmonious state has the qualities of fluidity and workability. It represents creative thinking, especially in terms of problem-solving.

The Inner Elements: Fire

Schedule: Weeks 73–76.

Timing: About 45 minutes, once a day, six times a week.

Fire is imagined as a red tetrahedron in the centre of the body at the base of the throat. (A tetrahedron is like a three-sided pyramid. It has four faces, each in the shape of an equilateral triangle.) The tetrahedron sits on one of its sides with the point facing upwards. Fire in its harmonious state has the qualities of warmth and vitality.

The Inner Elements: Space

Schedule: Weeks 77–80.

Timing: About 45 minutes, once a day, six times a week.

Space has no shape. You can think of space as being the context within which all the other elements are knowable. Space is imagined as a clear blue open sky all around and you should try to imagine that you are inseparable from the sky-space. Space in its harmonious state has the qualities of open-mindedness as well as being non-judgemental.

The Inner Elements: Integration

Schedule: Weeks 81–84.

Timing: About 45 minutes, once a day, six times a week.

For this exercise, contemplate each of the elements, one after another, in the same session. Spend between five and ten minutes on each element. The sequence that you should follow is: earth, air, water, fire, space.

The chart on page 156 might be helpful in exploring the qualities of the elements. It is interesting to note that the Chinese and Tibetan traditional medical practices, which are more than 2,000 years old, are centred on maintaining the proper relationship between the elements.

Element	Qualities	Physiological	Psychological	Colour/shape	Location
Earth	Solidity, stability, and heaviness.	Solid matter: bones, hair, nails, solid fibre of flesh.	Balanced: stable, reliable. Too strong: heavy, sleepy, stubborn. Too weak: ungrounded.	Golden yellow cube.	Navel.
Water	Cohesion, adaptability, creativity, wetness and flow.	Body fluids and circulation: in, out and throughout the body.	Balanced: adaptable, creative, confident of solutions to problems. Too strong: excessively subjective. Too weak: easily panicked by minor problems; lacking confidence; afraid of feeling.	White sphere.	Heart.
Fire	Warmth, brightness and reactivity.	Heat of the body; sex hormones and adrenals.	Balanced: warm, loving, intuitive, clear-minded, generous and compassionate. Too strong: aggressive, emotional, passionate excess. Too weak: a cold, dark outlook, lacking warmth.	Ruby-red tetrahedron.	Base of throat.
Air	Movement, quickness and intelligence.	Nervous system: intellect.	Balanced: intelligent, keeps system in motion. Too strong: overactive, workaholic, anxious, fantasiser. Too weak: fatigued, listless, unwilling to think things through.	Green half-sphere.	Pelvic girdle.
Space	Infinite openness, unobstructed, all-pervading.	Spaces in the body but more mind-related.	Balanced: open-minded, able to experience 'non-solid' reality without losing touch with relative reality. Too strong: spaced-out, unable to relate to ordinary things and events. Too weak: claustrophobic, crowded, confused mind.	Deep blue, formless.	No specific location.

Universal Compassion

Schedule: Weeks 85–88.

Timing: About 45 minutes, once a day, six times a week.

This exercise is similar to 'The Healing Lights' exercise, which concentrated on the need for healing. In this exercise, your capacity to bring that same healing quality to the world is explored.

Seeking a Statement of Compassion (the first week)

Each day, do one of the previous exercises that you are particularly fond of. Choose the exercise that has brought you the most personal benefit and/or has had the greatest positive impact on your working relationship with others. In particular, choose the exercise that has left you with the warmest feeling towards the other people who you work with. You can do a different exercise each day or the same one for the entire week.

Each day at the conclusion of the exercise, and before you return to your normal activities, spend 15–20 minutes contemplating the nature of compassion in your own life. Think about the compassion that other people have shown towards you. Think about the good, decent things that you have done for other people and for yourself. Think about how good this has made you feel and how good it has made other people feel.

During the course of the week, use your journal to write your statement of compassion. It can be of any length or content. It should reflect at your most personal level what compassion means to you. It can be in your own words or in someone else's. If you like, it can be a statement from your religion. It can also be a statement from a famous person, a philosopher or great thinker who you respect and believe in. Most important, however, is that you identify with it. This is you, this is who you are and who you aspire to be.

The following statement of compassion, called *The Four*

Limitless Meditations comes from the Buddhist tradition. It is just a sample of what you might want to use or create:

> *May all beings have happiness and the causes of happiness.*
> *May they all be free from suffering and the causes of suffering.*
> *May each one never be separate from the true happiness which has no suffering.*
> *May they always act with great impartiality, free from attachment to close ones and aversion to others.*

At the end of the week do something to preserve your statement in such a way that you can carry it around with you easily and where you are likely to see it often throughout the week. You could write or print it on a card and laminate it, for example. Most personal time management software packages have a section for keeping your goals and values and you may want to enter it there.

Developing the Compassionate Aspiration (weeks two to four)

Begin the exercise in a seated position with your back straight. Spend a few minutes doing the 'Breathing' exercise on pages 117–8, then relax until you can feel calm. Now read your statement of compassion. If you like, read it out loud; you might even want to memorise it. Read it carefully, noting what it means to you. Then spend the next 15 minutes contemplating its meaning to you. Concentrate on developing a sense of compassion and loving kindness towards yourself and those around you. Note any personal pain or joy that you are experiencing. Then think about the people around you. Start with the people who are closest to you, then others who are less close. Develop a wish that everyone can experience the same sort of joy that you are experiencing; and that no one ever suffers the particular kinds of pain that you are experiencing.

Once you have a strong sense that these feelings are present in you, relax for a minute, experiencing this sense in a non-verbal, non-analytic fashion. Now imagine that in front of you in space there are three horizontal bands of colour. All three bands are of equal width and span the entire horizon. They are semi-translucent, like a rainbow, not solid. The top band of colour is a brilliant diamond-clear white; the middle band a rich ruby red; the bottom band a deep sky blue. These bands of light are the universal manifestation of compassion in its three forms: body, speech and mind. This is the universal compassion, both realised and potential, that is present in all of us. These bands of light radiate pure, uncontrived compassion and loving kindness.

The white band radiates pure, uncontrived compassion associated with the body. (White light heals the physical body.) The red light radiates pure, uncontrived compassion associated with speech. The blue light radiates pure, uncontrived compassion associated with mind. The white light enters the body through the forehead; the red light at the base of the throat; the blue light at the heart-centre. The lights permeate the body, turning it into a translucent rainbow of colours. As they spread through your body, contemplate the number of times in your life when you wanted to act compassionately but lacked either the wisdom or the will to do so. Perhaps you were afraid of personal loss; perhaps you were too preoccupied with your own suffering; perhaps you did not recognise the suffering of others; perhaps you tried but your actions were ineffectual.

As the light permeates your body, imagine that all your aspirations and unrealised potential for compassionate thoughts and deeds are transformed into pure actuality. The lights dissolve all the constraints of body, speech and mind. There is nothing limiting you. You are limitless compassion and loving kindness. Everything you do, everything you think, everything you desire is fully actualised compassion and loving kindness. Spend 15 to 30 minutes in this contemplation.

After developing some sense of this embodiment of compassion and loving kindness, turn your attention gently to the world around you. Note without judging what you see, what you hear, what you smell, what you touch. Everything that you sense becomes permeated by the rainbow lights, taking on the uncontrived compassionate qualities of the three bands of colours.

Everything you see has the pure qualities of compassion; everything you hear is the sound of compassion. Recognise that every thought, every memory, every idea has the inherent capacity to be transformed into compassionate action. In front of you and all around you the three bands of light emanate this joyous compassionate essence to everyone and everything. The three bands of white, red and blue glow with radiant energy.

If at first something strikes you as unpleasant, recognise its capacity to strip away all your negativity. Recognise it as an opportunity to generate positive qualities of patience, wisdom and understanding. Maintain this contemplation for 15 to 30 minutes.

At the conclusion of the session the three bands of light dissolve into space. Imagine, however, that their presence is still with you and with the world around you. Spend a few minutes relaxing and returning to your present situation. Carry as much as possible of this sensation of well-being with you into your day-to-day activities. In particular, carry the understanding that you have the skills, aspirations and energy to act compassionately towards yourself and those around you.

Retreats and Support Services

Relaxation Retreat

The retreat schedule on page 162 is appropriate for a three-day relaxation retreat and is designed to accompany the section on retreats in Part 1 (pages 80–90). This type of retreat can be done by anyone, whether or not they are following the scheduled exercise sessions.

Environment

Select somewhere appealing to the senses such as a mountain cabin or a beach. Find a location that is relatively isolated, somewhere where you won't be meeting people. If this is impossible, select a location away from home such as a friend's house. Make sure that the environment inside is clean and orderly. You don't want to be looking at clutter or dust while you are trying to relax.

Supplies

Warm, comfortable, very loose-fitting clothes, including jacket and warm socks.
Good walking shoes, preferably waterproof.
Blanket or yoga pad for floor work.
Massage oil.
Art supplies – any or all of the following: paper, paints, brushes,

rags for cleaning, board to put paper on, clay, spoons, knives, scissors, poster paper, poster paint, old plastic tubs for water and paint mixing, rubber bands and paper clips, markers and pencils.

Food

If you are in a group, the facilitators will provide for this but you might also want to consider bringing some dried fruit or vegetables. Avoid salty, greasy foods such as chips or processed snacks. No fizzy drinks or alcohol either. Cigarettes are definitely out.

If you are doing the retreat alone, then prepare as much of the food as possible in advance. Choose nutritious foods that are easy to digest. You might want to avoid meat and dairy foods to give your body a holiday too.

If you cook, make sure that your preparations are simple. If possible, choose a single-dish meal such as a large salad, a casserole, or a soup with some bread.

	Day One	Day Two	Day Three	Day Four
6 am		Get up, bathe. Add a break to the routine – don't shave, don't use make-up, don't blow-dry hair. Maintain silence.	(As Day Two.)	(As Day Two.)
6.30 am		Contemplative walk, weather permitting. No talking; appreciate your surroundings	(As Day Two.)	(As Day Two.)
8 am		Breakfast & clean-up. Quiet conversation permitted.	(As Day Two.)	(As Day Two.)

ENLIGHTENED MANAGEMENT

	Day One	Day Two	Day Three	Day Four
9 am		'Breathing' exercise. Contemplate feelings. Freeform artwork alone.	(As Day Two.)	(As Day Two.)
9.45 am		Tea break	(As Day Two.)	(As Day Two.)
10.15 am		'Feeling' exercise, lying on floor.	'Golden Gate of Compassion' exercise.	
11 am		Bodywork – yoga, massage, creative movement.	(As Day Two.)	(As Day Two.)
12 am		'The Healing Lights – White Light' exercise.	'The Healing Lights – Red Light' exercise.	'The Healing Lights – Blue Light' exercise.
12.45 pm		Lunch & Break. Contemplative walk.	(As Day Two.)	(As Day Two.)
2 pm		'The Outer Elements – Earth' exercise.	'The Outer Elements – Air' exercise.	'The Outer Elements – Water' exercise.
3.15 pm		'The Inner Elements – Earth' exercise.	'The Inner Elements – Air' exercise.	'The Inner Elements – Water' exercise.
4 pm		Tea break.	(As Day Two.)	(As Day Two.)
4.30 pm		Artwork – group work if possible.	(As Day Two.)	(As Day Two.)
6 pm	Arrival: prepare site; clean and make it attractive. Put away everything and pre-prepare food.	Dinner & break.	(As Day Two.)	Dinner and departure.
8 pm	'Breathing' & 'Golden Gate of Compassion' exercise.	(As Day One.)	(As Day One.)	

	Day One	Day Two	Day Three	Day Four
8.30 pm	Relax, sit by fire or outside; glass of beer or wine permitted.	Write journal. Do 'Clarifying Blame' exercise. Contemplative time.	(As Day Two.)	
10 pm	Lights out.	(As Day One.)	(As Day One.)	

Self-work Support Groups

Contact one of the service providers (below) for a list of support groups in your area or for assistance in starting up your own group.

Service Providers

The following organisations have been approved by Dr Akong Tulku Rinpoche to provide support for the self-work contemplations, exercises and techniques presented here. They can provide a range of services including:

Relaxation retreats.
Project and team retreats and services.
Individual coaching.
Self-work support groups.

Tara Associates
Thorn Lea House
32 Grappenhall Road
Stockton Heath
Cheshire
WA 2AG
UK
EMail: diana@taraassoc.u-net.com
Tel/fax: +44 1925 268322

Tara Associates
PO Box 360866
Columbus, Ohio 43236
USA
EMail: DonaWitten@aol.com